THE TECHNIQUE OF HONITON LACE

THE TECHNIQUE OF HONITON LACE

Elsie Luxton

B T Batsford Ltd
London

To my daughter Pauline

© Elsie Luxton 1979
First published 1979
Reprinted 1979, 1980, 1982, 1987, 1990

ISBN 0 7134 1614 9

Filmset in 'Monophoto' Century Schoolbook by
Servis Filmsetting Ltd, Manchester

Designed by Ken Williamson

Printed in Great Britain by
Courier International Ltd, Tiptree, Essex
for the publishers B. T. Batsford Ltd
4 Fitzhardinge Street, London W1H 0AH

Contents

The author working Honiton lace

Introduction

When I was five years old, my grandmother, Susannah Tedbury, of Aylesbeare, Devon, gave me her large bolster lace pillow and her lace bobbins and taught me the basic stitches of Honiton lace. Later, as a pupil of Clyst Honiton village school near Exeter, I studied the craft from the age of eight under the tutorship of Miss Effie Kempe, lace adviser to Devon County Council Education Committee. She was an excellent lacemaker and teacher, and created many lovely designs – and one especially for me. The photograph of the Roses and Lilies Floral Mat, pattern **41**, shows this design, of which I worked four mats (using No. 250 cotton – a fine thread that is no longer obtainable), which were designed to fit onto a silver tray as a base for the four-piece silver tea set I had won in a competition. After leaving school I continued to study lacemaking under the guidance of Mrs Whitakker, who had succeeded Miss Kempe as lace adviser. She also was a very experienced lacemaker and taught lacemaking in Devon for fifty years.

In 1955 I began teaching lace myself, at Cullompton, Bradninch, Exeter, Exmouth, Topsham, Broadhembury and Broadclyst. Together with Mrs Joyce Chambers I was tutor of the first residential course on Honiton lacemaking held at Exmouth in 1966, organised by the National Federation of Women's Institutes. This course proved so popular that it became an annual event, and is now organised by the Devon Federation of Women's Institutes. Largely as a result of this course's success, Devon teachers are now in demand by educational authorities to teach the art of Honiton lacemaking throughout the country, and I have taken courses for the College of Craft Education at King Alfred College, Winchester, West Dean College, Chichester, and for many other establishments in Britain and Europe.

The most memorable pieces of lace which I have made over the years include one of the six lace-edged handkerchiefs presented to Princess Margaret as a wedding gift in 1962, the lace-edged handkerchief presented to the Dowager Duchess of Gloucester during one of the Devon County Shows, and the wedding veil with eight yards of Brunswick edging which I made during the 1950s. This veil was displayed at the Women's Institute County Exhibition in Devon in

9

Wedding veil made by the author

1960 and National Exhibition in London in 1961, at the Triennial Conference of the Associated Countrywomen of the World in Melbourne in 1962, and at an exhibition in Rennes, Exeter's twin city in France, in 1966. The veil was also worn by my daughter at her wedding in 1974.

After sixty years of involvement with lacemaking, my aim is to keep this traditional Devon craft alive. Honiton lace has often been described as the finest of the English hand-made laces, yet there are very few textbooks on this craft, and none has been published in recent years. It is in response to the demand from my students, and to meet the great revival of interest in hand-lacemaking throughout Britain, that this book has been written. Practical instructions for 52 traditional and modern designs have been included, ranging from a beginner's first pattern to pieces using the most advanced techniques. It covers flat work, raised and rolled work, and includes an excellent selection of the filling stitches and leaf patterns which form such an attractive feature of this type of lace.

Not the least of the pleasures that lacemaking has given me for many years is the friendship that I have gained from so many people, both at home and abroad, through the art of lacemaking, and this gives me the opportunity to thank them all most sincerely. I appreciate the kindness they have extended to me.

I also wish to express my thanks to three of my students who have given me valuable assistance with this book: Cynthia Voysey, who helped with the art work, Patricia Philpott, who did the photography, and Susanne Thompson for her help with the script. Mrs Bishop of Dawlish, Devon, designed the Sampler and Convolvulus Panel, Cynthia Voysey worked the Sampler, and all the other lace I have worked myself, 27 of these pieces being my own designs.

1 ⠶ The History of Honiton Lace

Honiton lace is the most famous of all English hand-made bobbin laces; it is also the finest and the most expensive.

Throughout the Middle Ages, English seaports were visited by mercantile vessels from the Netherlands, trading woven cloth for British wool. It was largely due to these close trading ties that, during the intensely cruel religious persecutions by the Spanish Duke of Alva in the second half of the sixteenth century, large numbers of Flemish refugees fled to England. Many of them settled along the east and south Devon coast, in towns and villages from Beer to Torquay, where the women introduced the making of Flemish pillow lace. Devonians, however, were already making bone lace, so called because lacemakers then wound their threads onto small bones as bobbins and used fish bones to fasten the lace to the pillow. Thus, the English and Flemish skills combined to give us Honiton lace as we know it today; around the east Devon district the lace trade flourished for 400 years.

In Queen Anne's reign (1702–1714) Honiton lace became an article of currency, being used in Scotland to finance the Jacobite rebellions. There is no doubt that lace of a sort was made in Britain for a very long time before the arrival of the Flemish lacemakers in England. This early lace was a darned net; in the inventory of Exeter Cathedral for the year 1327 three pieces of darned net for use on the altar are mentioned. This type of net lace is to be found in the Cathedral on a monument to Bishop Stafford, who died in 1398. Early bone lace can also be seen on the sculptured figure of Lady Doddridge over her tomb in the Cathedral; she died in 1614. A collar of Honiton lace also adorns the stone effigy of Elizabeth Pole, wife of Sir John Pole; she died in 1638. Also, in Farway Church near Honiton, a collar and cuffs of Honiton lace are depicted on a stone effigy of a member of the Prideaux family.

Among the great lace merchants of Honiton was one James Rodge, who sent large quantities of lace abroad. When he died in 1617 he was buried in the churchyard of St Michaels, Honiton, where the burial register contains many names of lace merchants in the seventeenth and eighteenth centuries. In 1724 there were about 3600 lacemakers in Devon, of whom at least half resided in Honiton.

Queen Charlotte, wife of George III (1760–1820), ordered a dress of Honiton lace from a Mrs Davey who ran a lace shop in Honiton. The original sprigs of lace were mounted on hand-made net, the art of making which has alas been lost for ever. The lace was collected from the workers by agents who took it to Honiton; from there it was sent to the London dressmakers; thus it became known as Honiton lace, although it was actually made in many parts of Devon.

In the 1760s a form of net was produced on the stocking frame and by the 1780s an improved version called 'Point Net' was becoming widely used. More important, however, was the bobbin net machine patented in 1809 by Thomas Heathcoat. At that time he bought a factory at Tiverton, Devon, and started to produce machine lace.

During the early nineteenth century changes in fashion brought about a decrease in the demand for hand-made lace; as a result, the number of lace workers dwindled year by year. Pay was so poor that the Honiton lace workers began using inferior patterns and techniques, using less threads to produce more lace. Thus Honiton lace lost its charm and quality during this period. Payment was made by the barter system, the lace workers being given tea, sugar and other commodities in exchange for their lace. The depressed lace workers eventually sought Royal favour, and as a result Queen Adelaide (wife of William IV) ordered a complete dress to be made of Honiton lace sprigs, expressing a wish that the design should be formed of flowers copied from nature, and that the initial letter of each flower should form the name of the Queen, i.e. Amaranth, Daphne, Eglantine, Lilac, Auricula, Ivy and Dahlia.

Beer, on the east Devon coast, became one of the main centres of the revived industry, and it was here that in 1840 the wedding dress of Queen Victoria was made. The order was given to a Jane Bidney who gathered together one hundred of the best lacemakers for the task; the number of workers had diminished so much that it was difficult to find really good ones. The lace cost £1000, quite a large sum in those days. Queen Victoria often visited Sidmouth, and helped to establish once again the fashion for the famous Devon lace. She ordered a black lace shawl from the lacemakers of Beer; the sprigs were made of silk and mounted on machine-made silk net. Black lace had not been made in Devon for a great number of years owing to the expense of the silk, which cost double the price of linen thread; samples of this black lace are very rare today.

Since that period, the Honiton lace industry has been fortunate in having the patronage of many members of the Royal Family. On the occasion of the Coronation of King George VI and Queen Elizabeth, a Honiton lace fan was presented to the Queen by the people of Honiton. Mrs Allen, who until a few years ago had a lace shop in Beer, made a handkerchief for Queen Elizabeth in 1939. Princess Elizabeth, now the Queen, was presented with a lace-mounted cocktail tray as a twenty-first birthday gift from the women of Honiton, while Mrs Dowell of Branscombe made a piece of lace at the age of 90 which the Queen accepted in 1951.

Other Devon laces, Trolly and Branscombe Point, were made in the nine-teenth century. The Trolly lace was worked in a continuous length, the parchment pattern being pinned round the pillow to enable the lacemaker to work long lengths without having to 'lift' the lace; this is very similar to the English Midlands laces. Branscombe Point was made with either hand-made or machine-made braids. These were pinned or stitched to a fabric pattern, the sections between the braids being made with the needle; these filling stitches had names such as Holly, Purl Zig-Zag, Wheatsheaf, Butterfly, etc. Black Branscombe Point lace was made and used for evening coats in the early years of the twentieth century. This Point lace was much quicker and easier to make than Honiton lace, and was therefore much in demand, being so much cheaper. No Trolly lace is now made in Devon, the art having been lost, but a little Branscombe Point is still made in Branscombe.

Before compulsory education came into force in many parts of Devon, children from the age of five were sent to lace schools. It is surprising what clean and accurate work they turned out; later in life they were often the best lacemakers. Their first patterns were called 'Slugs' and later patterns called 'Cottage Loaves' were made; many of these patterns can often be seen on old wedding veils. Men, women and also boys of all ages went to these lace schools, many working twelve hours a day, often by oil lamps. Many young women who were delicate or otherwise unfit for domestic service were able to support themselves by working in the lace schools, making, repairing and undertaking the general care of valuable lace which was sent to the school.

In the early part of the twentieth century pupils from a lace school at Shaldon, Devon, made a 'Tucker' for the Coronation of Queen Mary. At Honiton a Mrs Fowler ran a lace school in her own home; the ladies all wore black, and their lace was sent all over the world. The designer for some of the most beautiful patterns which were used was Mrs Ward (an aunt of Mrs Fowler); the Honeysuckle pattern in this book is one of Mrs Ward's designs. Mrs Goodman, who ran the lace shop at Honiton from 1929 to 1968, learnt her lace making at Mrs Fowler's school, and later took over the lace shop from her. The Devon County Education Committee has always taken a great interest in lacemaking and has voted several sums of money to aid in reviving and keeping this lovely craft alive.

At the beginning of the twentieth century many lace classes were run in Devon schools; the only one remaining is at Honiton, and it is conducted after school hours. However, many Adult Education Classes take place all over Devon. These are well supported, with interest growing all the time. The craft of lacemaking is one of the many traditional crafts that people with more leisure time are taking up today. It is a delicate and skilful craft which should be given every opportunity to remain part of our cultural and educational heritage for all time to come.

2 ⚃ Equipment and Preparation

EQUIPMENT

Honiton pillow

This should be round in shape. The correct way to work is to have the pillow on the knee and to rest it against a table edge. In working, it is often necessary to turn the pillow. Formerly, pillows were large and rather cumbersome; today a smaller pillow is generally used. Use strong cotton or linen fabric to make the pillow. The size can vary, but two circular pieces 33 cm to 36 cm (13 to 14 in.) in diameter are recommended and these should be joined by a straight strip 8 cm (3 in.) wide. Make strong seams and leave an opening for inserting the stuffing. The recommended stuffing is chopped straw, oat or barley straw for preference; wheat straw is rather coarse and will cause the fine lace pins to bend when inserted, unless it has first been cut into short lengths and had the knots in the stems removed. The pillow must be evenly packed, and should be hammered on top, between handfuls of stuffing, with a small, hard wooden mallet or rolling pin. The pillow must be very hard, so that the pins, when inserted, are held firmly; the firmer the pillow, the better the lace.

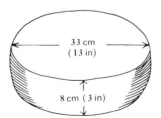

The lace pillow

Cover cloths

These are made of casement or linen fabric; a blue or dark green colour is restful to the eyes. If neither of these fabrics is available, the material from which cover cloths are made should be smooth and free from loose fibres, which might become worked into the lace. One metre (one yard) square can be cut into four pieces approximately 50 cm (18 in.) square. Three of these pieces should be hemmed to be used as cover cloths, and the fourth can be made into a bobbin case.

Bobbin case

As the bobbins are usually cut off from the pillow in pairs, a case will prevent them from becoming entangled with other pairs. The case is made from a piece of washable material, about 46 cm (18 in.) long (or longer if required) and 26 cm (10 in.) deep. Hem the piece all round. Turn one of the long sides up on the

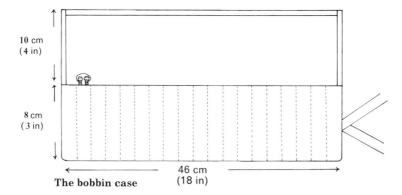

10 cm
(4 in)

8 cm
(3 in)

46 cm
(18 in)

The bobbin case

wrong side for about 8 cm (3 in.) and stitch pockets 2.5 cm (1 in.) wide to contain one pair of bobbins each. When the bobbins are in the case, the top edge of the material is folded down over them, and the whole thing is then rolled up from one end and tied round with tapes, which should be stitched on at the other end.

Pincushion

The use of a small pincushion, about 5 cm (2 in.) square or round, preferably stuffed with sheep's wool, is advisable. If the pins were put into the side of the pillow, they would have to be moved as the pattern progressed.

Thread

The fine Honiton lace cotton is gassed. Nos. 140, 180 and 200 are preferable when obtainable, but these fine threads are becoming very difficult to find. No. 120 mercerised cotton is suitable for beginners, as is a fine, unbleached cotton thread. For the 'coarse' cotton thread (gimp), used to outline and strengthen the lace, buy a good quality sewing cotton, No. 50 for the No. 120 lace thread, and a finer sewing cotton for use with the No. 180 lace thread, when this is available.

Pins

The special pins used for Honiton lace are fine white brass pins, somewhat shorter than ordinary pins. Berry pins, for pinning down the cover cloths, and a few dressmaking pins for pinning the pattern onto the pillow are also useful.

Needlepin

This little tool is used to take sewings, to shorten or lengthen the thread on the bobbins, etc. It can be made by driving a needle into a wooden handle 5 cm to 8 cm (2 to 3 in.) long. Use a No. 7 or 8 Sharps or Betweens needle and insert it into the handle so that the pointed end projects for about 2 cm ($\frac{3}{4}$ in.). This needlepin is too fragile for pricking patterns, and for this purpose another fine needlepin, with the needle projecting only 5 mm ($\frac{1}{4}$ in), is used.

Pricking card

Patterns are pricked on stiff, glazed card. Parchment was used in former times.

Scissors

Two pairs are necessary, one small pair with sharp points (e.g. embroidery or lace scissors) and one small *blunt* pair with sharp points.

Pricking board

A cork mat is best for making prickings; however, if this is unobtainable, patterns can be pricked on the lace pillow, particularly if it is a firm one.

Bobbins

These can be made of many woods – spindle, holly, ebony, box, etc. Three dozen are required initially, but as the student progresses, more will be needed. The Honiton bobbin is perfectly plain, smooth and light in weight, as the thread used is so fine. It has a grooved neck on which to wind the thread, a head to keep the thread in place, and a tapered tail, which is necessary for taking sewings and tying knots.

Sliders

Today these are made of perspex, plexiglass, or acetate; previously horn or talc was used. Two pieces approximately 12 cm by 6 cm ($4\frac{3}{4}$ by $2\frac{1}{2}$ in.) are needed. They are placed under and between the cover cloths, to prevent the threads from catching on the pins or the edges of the pattern.

Winder

Bobbins can be wound by hand, but sometimes an old winder can be found and this makes bobbin-winding quicker and easier.

PREPARATION

Winding bobbins

It is important that they should always be wound in the same direction: looking down on the head of the bobbin, wind the thread round clockwise. Hold the end of the thread against the neck of the bobbin until the first few turns have been made to keep it in place, then wind the bobbin evenly and firmly.

When the bobbin is full, a half-hitch must be made to prevent it from un-

The Honiton bobbin

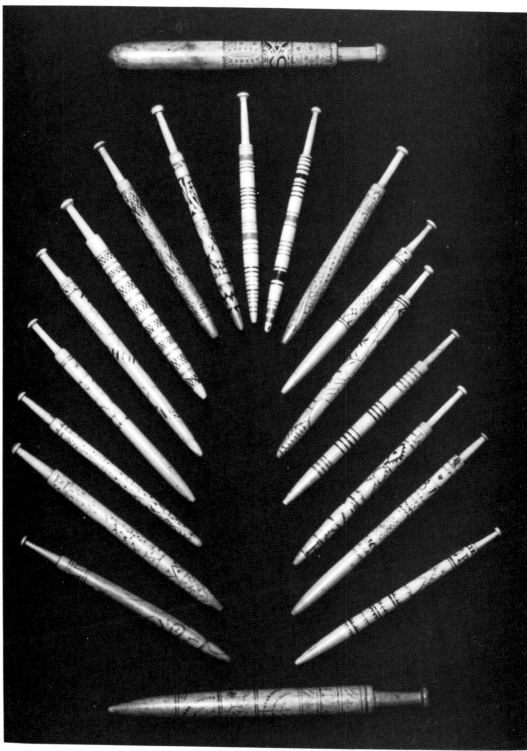

Antique Honiton lace bobbins

winding. Holding the bobbin and the end of the thread in the left hand, put the forefinger of the right hand under the thread from behind, with the palm towards you and the finger pointing down. Twist the finger away from the bobbin until the back of the hand faces you and there is a loop of thread round the finger. Put the top of the finger on the top of the bobbin, and slip this loop over the head of the bobbin onto the thread.

There is no need to wind Honiton bobbins in pairs without knots, as is usual for other laces; the bobbins are wound singly and tied into pairs afterwards using the scissors method, as follows.

Hold the pair of bobbins in the left hand, letting the ends of the thread pass loosely over the backs of the fingers and holding them under the little finger. Put the closed, blunt scissors between the threads and the back of the fingers, and twist the points of the scissors over the thread towards you and down under the threads, making a complete loop round the scissors. Open the scissors, and from underneath catch the portion of thread between the scissors and little finger. Close the scissors gently, and pull the points back through the loop, until this slips off the point and a new loop is held in the scissors. Cut this loop and pull away the cut ends of the thread. The bobbins come away tied together.

The half-hitch

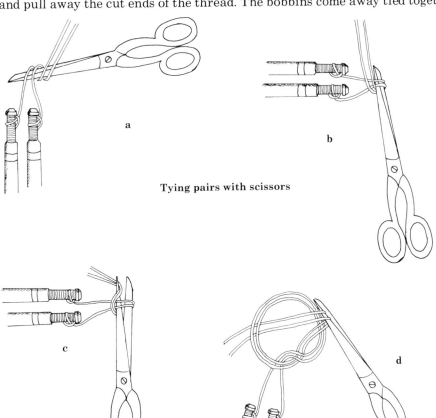

Tying pairs with scissors

Winding the knots back

Unhitch the thread from one of a pair of bobbins and wind the knot tying the pair together onto this bobbin. Replace the hitch. This can also be done by placing the needlepin into the back of the hitched loop, pulling gently and winding the bobbin towards you. With experience one can judge how far to wind the knot, according to the pattern to be worked and the stitch used – in the first pattern, the knots need only be wound just onto the bobbin. A knot should never be worked into the lace. Prepare one pair of bobbins wound with coarse thread.

The pricking

This is the lacemaking term used for the pattern over which the lace is worked. The prickings in this book are the actual size for working. Fasten a piece of tracing paper to the page over the pricking with paper clips, and, with a pencil, mark all the dots. Cut a piece of pricking card to the size needed for the pattern, lay the tracing on it, and fasten the two to the pricking board with drawing pins, or to the pillow with strong pins. With a needlepin or pricker, prick all the dots through onto the card, holding the pricker *vertically*, not slanted like a pencil. The holes must not be too big, or the pins will not be firm when the lace is being made. Great care should be taken that the holes are pricked accurately, as the finished appearance of the lace depends largely on a good pricking.

Dressing the pillow

Cover the pillow with one of the cover cloths, and pin the four corners down firmly under the pillow with berry pins. Pin the pricking onto the centre of the pillow with strong, flat-headed pins, one at each corner. Fold the two remaining cover cloths in half and place the folded edges facing each other over the pricking but not touching, so that a small portion of the pricking to be worked is exposed. Pin the cloths firmly with berry pins, low down on the sides of the pillow. Slip the sliders under these cover cloths, to lie on the pricking, one each side of the portion to be worked. Pin the pincushion on the pillow, using a long, strong pin like a hat pin.

3 ⁛ Beginners' Pieces

Although the patterns in this book are not progressive, the beginner should start by working patterns **1** and **2**, which are described in great detail and show most of the basic working methods. Also, it is advisable to work patterns **7**, **11** and **12** (which involve a lot of sewing) to gain some practice at taking sewings before attempting a piece of raised work. All patterns except pattern **1** have been worked in No. 180 cotton thread, and if a thicker thread is used, a corresponding adjustment must be made in the number of bobbins used. The numbers given here are meant to be used as a guide, and the worker will soon be able to judge how many pairs are required by the appearance of the braid being worked. The numbers in brackets refer to the notes in Chapter 9.

STITCHES
Basically only two very simple stitches are used, each requiring two pairs of bobbins. Do not number or mark the bobbins – they are continually changing position and it will only confuse you to do so.

The hands, while working, should be kept palm downwards. The bobbins in use should always be in the space actually in front of you. Care should be taken that the bobbins pushed aside are kept in the right order, as they can easily become displaced.

Whole stitch
To learn the stitch, think of the bobbins as being numbered 1, 2, 3 and 4, from left to right. With the left hand, lift 2 and lay it over 3. Now, using both hands, lift the new 2 and 4 simultaneously to the left over 1 and 3. Repeat the first

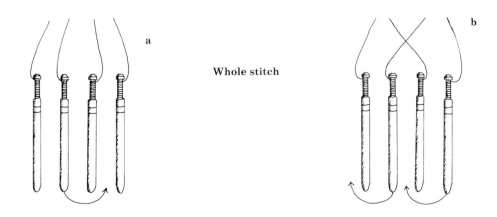

Whole stitch

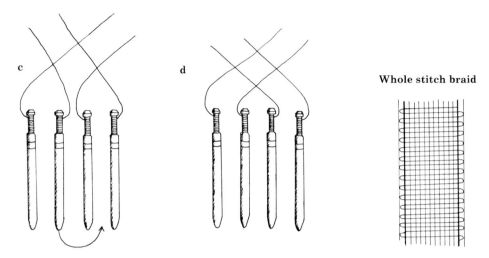

Whole stitch braid

movement, lifting 2 over 3 with the left hand. This completes one whole stitch. When a row of whole stitches has been made, the effect is that of two threads weaving across from one side to the other.

Half stitch

This is similar to whole stitch, except that the last movement is omitted. Place 2 over 3, then, using both hands, lift the new 2 and 4 over 1 and 3. This is the end of the stitch; when a row of half stitch is worked, only one thread weaves across and each pair is left twisted once.

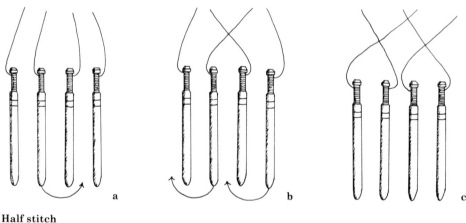

Half stitch

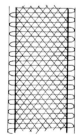

Half stitch braid

PATTERN 1: THREE-LEAF SPRAY

This pattern is worked in No. 120 cotton thread, with No. 50 sewing cotton as coarse thread.

Whole stitch leaf

The centre leaf is worked first. Instructions for starting a Honiton braid at a point are given in note **1a**, Chapter 9, but the process is more fully described here.

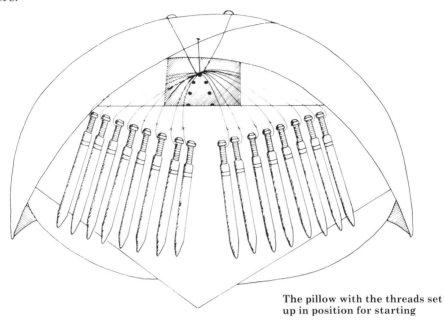

The pillow with the threads set up in position for starting

Pattern 1: Three-leaf Spray

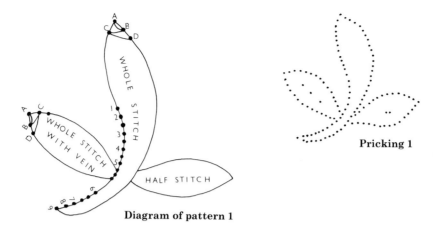

WHOLE STITCH

WHOLE STITCH WITH VEIN

HALF STITCH

Diagram of pattern 1

Pricking 1

Set a pin in hole A and hang eight pairs round it so that all the bobbins with the knots are in the middle, and there are four knot-free bobbins on the left and four knot-free bobbins on the right. Twist each two adjacent bobbins by placing the right-hand bobbin over the left-hand one twice. Take the pair wound with coarse thread, one bobbin in each hand, and slide the thread connecting them under the ten central bobbins, leaving two pairs on the left and one pair on the right, and lay it to the back of the pillow.

Work a whole stitch with the two outside pairs on the left, twist both pairs three times. * Push the left-hand pair to the left and leave. Bring the next pair from the right to join the remaining pair in front of you and make another whole stitch with these two pairs. Repeat from * across the row, until only one pair on the right remains unworked. It will be seen that the original outside pair on the left has woven through to the right. This pair is called the runner pair, or simply 'the runners', and the pairs the runners have passed through are called 'passives' or 'downrights'. Twist the runners three times (right over left), set a pin in hole B under these two threads and work a whole stitch with the runners and the last (edge) pair. Twist both these pairs three times.

Before working the next row, bring the coarse threads down into position, to lie third from the left and fifth from the right, making sure that this thread is brought down *inside* pin B. The coarse threads each make a pair with the next thread on the inside (called the 'coarse pair') and this pair is worked as an ordinary downright pair. Work the next row, using the second pair from the right as runners, leaving the former runners resting at the edge and making the first whole stitch with the coarse thread and its partner. * Push the right-hand pair of these two to the right and bring the next pair from the left to join the pair in front of you. Make another whole stitch and then repeat from *. Note that the movements of the whole stitch are not reversed – each stitch is made exactly as described above, in whichever direction it is being worked.

When all but the edge pair on the left have been worked, twist the runners three times, set pin C under them and work a whole stitch with the runners and edge pair. Twist both pairs three times. The inner of these pairs will now become the runners for the next row, and the next pin on the other side (D) will be set when the runners have passed through all except the last pair on the right and have been twisted three times. Before making the whole stitch with the edge pair, hang in a new pair (note **2a**). Continue working back and forth as above, hanging in one pair at each pin (both sides) until there are sixteen pairs altogether.

Continue the work until pin 1 has been set. Take the two bobbins next to the left-hand coarse thread on the inside and cut them off with the blunt scissors, so that they come away tied together (note **25**). This is called 'bowing off'. Trim the ends of thread close to the lace and continue work, taking out one pair at every hole on this side until nine pairs altogether remain. In addition, back stitches (note **4**) will be necessary at holes 2, 3 and 4, in order to keep the rows of weaving level, at a right angle to the edge. Continue the stem. Back stitch again at 6, also remove another pair, as soon as this pin has been set for the first time. After making the edge at 7, take the two bobbins next to the left-hand coarse thread and lay them to the back of the pillow. At 8 another back stitch must be made and another pair (the two bobbins next to the left-hand coarse thread) is laid back, when the pin has been set for the first time. This will enable the last pin, 9, to be set on the right, with all the downrights curving towards the left and keeping to the shape of this pattern. (If the stem had curved the other way, it would have been necessary to arrange the weaving so that the last pin could have been set on the left.)

The method of finishing at a point is explained in note **24** but it is repeated here for beginners.

After pin 9 has been set, the coarse bobbins are cut off short and the runners are worked through all remaining pairs without twisting, including the edge pair on the other side. Holding the bobbins tail to tail, tie the runners three times, making the knots as close as possible to the lace. Tie all the other pairs three times. Pick up all the bobbins except the outer pair on each side, in one hand, cross the outer pairs. Pick up one bobbin from each outer pair and tie these three times over the bunch, then repeat this tying with the remaining two outer bobbins.

Press the first pin right down into the pillow, then remove every alternate pin and press the remainder down into the pillow, leaving the last two pins on each side standing up. Turn the pillow. The two pairs laid back must now be spread out, so that one bobbin of each pair lies on each side of the stem. Pick up all the other bobbins and bring them back over the stem, guiding the threads carefully between the standing pins, and lay them between the bobbins of the spread-out pairs. Tie these separately three times over the bunch. Cut off. Press pin 9 down into the pillow and either remove or press down the remaining standing pins.

Veined leaf

The left-hand leaf is worked similarly to the first leaf, in whole stitch, but it has a vein down the middle, made by twisting the runners three times in the centre of the row. However, as the pin holes are pricked slightly differently, it is more convenient to begin by working the first row from right to left, otherwise the rows of weaving would be slanted instead of level. Note that in this case, the pairs must be hung round pin A with four knot-free bobbins on the outside *right* and two on the outside *left*.

The twisting for the vein is started after two pairs have been hung in. Divide the downright into two, take the runners through the first section of downrights, twist them three times and continue working to the end of the row. Twist the runners at the same place in each row and ensure that the new pairs are added evenly so that there is an equal number of downrights on each side of the vein. This leaf requires 15 pairs in all. When taking out pairs where the leaf narrows, remove a pair from one side in one row and from the other side in the next row until only 8 pairs remain to work the stem end of the leaf. When about two holes on each side remain to be worked, close the vein by taking the runners straight across without twisting them in the middle. Take out one more pair. When the last hole has been used, work one more row through all pairs except the edge pair on the other side. Lay back the coarse threads. There are three holes in the edge of the stem opposite to the end of the leaf, to which the threads can be joined by means of sewings (note **20a**). In this case two pairs can be sewn into each hole of the stem.

After sewing, tie all pairs three times, bunch the bobbins, cross the two outer pairs under the bunch and tie them three times over the bunch, as at the end of the first leaf. Cut off the bobbins and trim the ends short, being careful not to cut into the knots holding this bunch. Cut off coarse threads close to the work. There is no need here to tie the bunched bobbins back over the leaf, as the cut ends of thread will be hidden under the stem when the spray is taken off the pillow and turned to its right side.

Half stitch leaf

Wind the knots connecting the bobbins a little further back, as knots in half stitch are awkward to manage. The leaf is begun and worked (in whole stitch) exactly as the first leaf, until pin B has been set, the edge stitch made, and the coarse threads have been brought down into position. With the second pair from the right, work a whole stitch with the coarse pair, twist the runners (the left of these two pairs) once and continue in half stitch. This is worked in the same way as whole stitch, that is, after each half stitch is made, lay aside the right-hand pair and bring down the next pair from the left to join the pair in front of you and make another half stitch. Continue working until only the coarse pair on the other side and the edge pair remain unworked. Then work a whole stitch with the runners and coarse pair, twist the runners three times, set pin C and work the normal whole stitch and three twists with the edge pair. Again, take the runners through the coarse pair in whole stitch, twist the runners once and continue in half stitch, this time laying the left pair aside after each half stitch and taking a new pair from the right. Work until two pairs remain unworked, make a whole stitch with the runners and coarse pair, twist runners three times and set pin D under them. Hang in a new pair at this hole (note **2b**) and at every following hole on each side until there are 15 pairs altogether.

Continue without further addition. When working towards the fifth hole from the bottom on the left-hand side, work as normal until three pairs remain unworked. Work through the next two pairs (i.e. the downright pair inside the coarse pair and the coarse pair) in whole stitch, twist the runners three times, set the pin and make the usual edge stitch and three twists. Before returning, take the two bobbins next to the coarse thread (i.e. the two middle bobbins of the two whole stitches), tie them three times close to the lace and cut them off. Work to the other side, again working two whole stitches at the end of the row before setting the pin and working the edge stitch. Then tie and cut off the two bobbins inside the right-hand coarse thread. Continue in half stitch, taking out one pair at each pin hole as above, until only seven pairs altogether remain.

When the last pin hole has been used, work one more row in whole stitch through all bobbins except the edge pair on the other side. Lay back the coarse threads and sew out the remaining six pairs, sewing two pairs into each of the nearest holes of the stem, and finish as for the last leaf.

PATTERN 2: SIMPLE ROSE WITH LEAVES AND RIB

Begin this pattern at the base of the stem according to note **1a**, using the second diagram. After three rows, add one pair (note **2a**) at each of the next two holes on the outer side of the curve of the stem – 9 pairs in all, to work up the stem. It will be necessary to back stitch (note **4**) three times at 1, 2 and 3 on the inner

Pattern 2: Simple Rose with Leaves and Rib

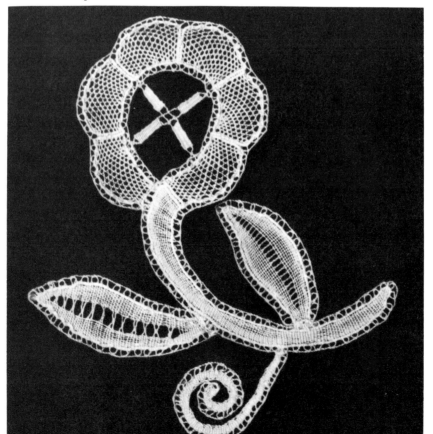

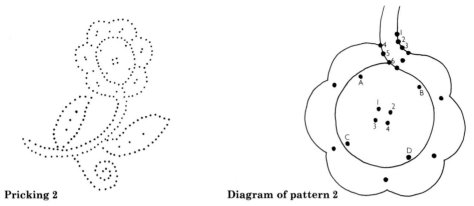

Pricking 2   **Diagram of pattern 2**

side of the stem where it runs into the flower, and add one pair at each of the three holes on the left at 4, 5 and 6 (see diagram). Also tie the runners (note **5**) at one or two holes on the left, where the stem bends sharply.

Cross the coarse thread (note **15**) at the place marked by the central hole and change to half stitch. The rest of the flower is completed in half stitch, with the coarse thread crossed between petals. It will be necessary to back stitch frequently on the inner side, in order to keep the work level; it is a good plan, after the coarse thread has been crossed, to count the holes on both sides as far as the next division, in order to work out how many back stitches are necessary. Sew out into the beginning of the flower, following the instructions in note **23**.

The leaves are worked as for the first pattern – one is whole stitch with a vein made by twisting the runners, the other is whole stitch with a ladder trail vein (see leaf **7**, Chapter 8), which is opened after three or four rows have been worked and closed three or four holes from the bottom of the leaf. Sew out into the stem.

Ribbed tendril

Use seven pairs. Begin at the tip of the tendril and work according to the instructions in note **18**. The pin hole side in this case is on the right. Sew out into the stem.

Filling

This is a fragment of Diamond filling, but it is described here for the sake of convenience.

Sew two pairs (note **20c**) into two adjacent edge holes of the flower above A and two pairs above B. With each two pairs make a whole stitch, twist all pairs three times and set pins A and B between each two pairs, which are then used to make a narrow leadwork (note **8**) to reach to the group of holes in the middle of the space. After making the first leadwork, twist both pairs three times and lay aside, making sure that the weaver thread remains slack; then work the second leadwork and twist both pairs three times. Set pins 1 and 2 between each two pairs, still keeping the weaver in each set loose. With the two middle pairs

of the four, work a whole stitch and twist both pairs three times. With the two
left-hand pairs work a whole stitch and twist both pairs three times and set
pin 3 between them. With the two right-hand pairs work a whole stitch, twist
both pairs three times and set pin 4 between them. With the two middle pairs
work a whole stitch and twist each pair three times. With the two left-hand
pairs work another leadwork to C, twist both pairs three times and set pin C
between them. Enclose the pin with a whole stitch and three twists. With the
two pairs remaining in the middle, make a leadwork to D, twist both pairs three
times, set pin D between them and enclose the pin with a whole stitch and three
twists. Sew out (note **20d**) both sets into adjacent holes below C and D.

PATTERN 3: SHELL

Centre braid

Set up (note **1a**) at 1 with six pairs and the coarse pair, and add (note **2a**) one
pair at 2 and 3. The whole of the centre braid is worked with these nine pairs.
It will be necessary to backstitch (note **4**) about nine times on the inner side of
the small circle in order to keep the work level. When approaching the beginning, back stitches will have to be made on the inside of the curve.

   After hole 4 has been worked and the edge stitch and twists have been
made, join by sewing the outside pair to 4. Replace pin 4 and work to the other
side. Work back towards 2. After passing through the coarse pair at the end of
the row, do not twist the runners but work a whole stitch through the edge pair;
then sew the runners to 2. Replace pin 2. Work through the edge pair again
without twists and continue to the other side. A similar join is made at 1, but
in this case take the sewing with the pin still in the hole, putting the needlepin
down beside the pin and bringing it out under the six loops which hang round
the pin. Although rather difficult to do, this is necessary, otherwise the pin hole
will be lost.

   After this sewing work a whole stitch with the two edge pairs, twist both
three times and continue work. The dots in the middle of the braid on the
diagram indicate the extent of the vein, which is made by twisting the runners
in the middle of the downrights. Where the braid approaches the completed
part it should be joined according to note **20e** at the four holes indicated on the
diagram. On reaching the position where the outside braid begins, hang in two
pairs (note **21**) at each of the four holes indicated on the diagram, and lay these
pairs aside. Sew out according to note **23**.

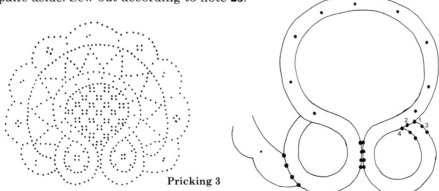

Pricking 3

Diagram of pattern 3

Outer braid

Tie once each of the pairs that were hung in for this braid. Put aside two pairs on the left and one pair on the right to be the runners. Weave the coarse pair under and over through the pairs remaining in the middle. Lay the coarse threads to the back of the pillow. Work a whole stitch and three twists with the two pairs on the left, and with the inner of these pairs work across in whole stitch to the other side, twist the runners three times, set the first pin under them, add a new pair (note **2a**) and work a whole stitch with the edge pair which should first have been twisted three times. Bring the coarse threads down into position, ensuring that the right-hand thread is placed inside the pin just set.

Pattern 3: Shell

Change to half stitch braid (note **1b**). Begin working the purl edge at the next hole on the right (note **9**) and also add a new pair (note **2c**) before making the first purl. On the inner side, back stitching will start immediately, and it is a good plan to count the number of pin holes on each side as far as the next crossing of the coarse threads (indicated by a single dot in the middle of the braid), in order to determine how many back stitches have to be made.

After crossing of the coarse thread (note **15**), change to whole stitch, add in another new pair inside the next purl. The four pin bud is worked according to note **11**. Continue working the braid, alternating whole stitch and half stitch with four pin bud all the way round, and sew out into the first braid. The fillings are Purl Pin Bars (filling **18**) and Four Pin (filling **6**).

PATTERN 4: SUNFLOWER

Stem and flower
Set up at the base of the stem (note **1a**) and add one pair (note **2a**) at each of the next two holes on the right to work the stem. Work back stitches at the last two or three holes on the right at the end of the stem (note **4**), in order to allow the braid to swing round into the flower. At the last three holes on the left before the braid turns, add one pair, and also tie the runners (note **5**) at the last of these holes. Change to half stitch for the flower, crossing the coarse thread (note **15**) where indicated. Sew out at beginning of flower (note **23**). The rib tendril is worked according to note **18** (seven pairs).

Divided leaf
The new feature in this pattern is the divided leaf, with whole stitch on one side and half stitch on the other. Sew seven pairs into the main stem (note **20c**) and work rib (note **18**) with pin holes on the left side, to make stem up to the leaf. Weave a coarse pair through all the downrights except the last pair on the

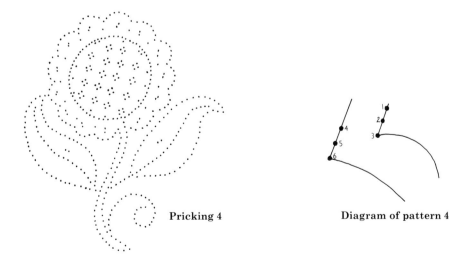

Pricking 4   Diagram of pattern 4

Pattern 4: Sunflower

plain side of the rib. Lay the coarse pair to the back of the pillow. The last pair on the plain side should be twisted three times and becomes the edge pair runner on this side. Work the runners through from the other side in whole stitch, add a pin and make the usual edge stitch. Bring the coarse threads down into position, ensuring that the thread on the side on which the pin has just been set lies inside the pin. Change to half stitch and gradually add pairs (note **2b**) on the outer side until there are fifteen pairs in all. Where the leaf narrows towards the point, gradually reduce the number of pairs to eight (note **3b**). To turn the top of the leaf, refer to the instructions for leaf **1**, Chapter 8.

The second side is worked in whole stitch. Near the end, it will be necessary to sew twice into each vein hole, so that when the last hole on the outer side has been worked, there are still two vein holes free and these may be used to sew the pairs out. By this time the number of pairs should have been reduced (note **3a**) to about five. After the last hole on the outer side has been made up, work the runners through to the other side, sew them into the upper of the two free vein holes, tie them three times and leave. Lay back the coarse threads and sew the nearest downright pair into the same hole as the runners and tie it three times. Sew and tie the runners on the outer edge and also the remaining pairs into the other vacant vein hole. Cut off the coarse threads, bunch and tie as usual and cut off. The other leaf is worked in a similar way. The filling is Diamond (filling **1**).

PATTERN 5: CENTRE ROSE AND THREE-LEAF SPRAYS

The rose
Begin by working the whole stitch ring at the centre of the flower, setting up at 1 with six pairs and the coarse pair (note **1a**) and working first towards the left. Remember to tie the runners (note **5**) at holes 2 and 4. Complete the circle, finishing the runners at the right-hand side. Sew the runners and right edge

Pricking 5

Diagram of pattern 5

Pattern 5: Centre Rose and Three-leaf Sprays

pair into hole 1 (note **20f**). One of the central downrights is sewn into hole 2 and the edge pair on the inner side into hole 4. After sewing, lay the outer right-hand pair aside to the right and lay the coarse threads back temporarily. Bunch the downright bobbins, cross the two sewn outer pairs under the bunch, and tie them three times over the bunch. Move the bunch of threads to the right and sew one of the pairs that were tied over the bunch into hole 1 to be one of the two runner pairs. Bring the coarse threads back into position (as the third thread on each side). Begin the petal by taking the sewn runner pair in whole stitch through all pairs except the pair put aside on the right (which should be twisted three times), twist runners three times and work the usual edge stitch at 5.

Work the runners back through three pairs, leave the runners and with the last pair they worked through as new runners, work towards 6. Add pin 6 and one new pair (note **2a**). Change to half stitch, working through to the inner side, where the runners are sewn. Continue working half stitch braid, adding a new pair at 7 and 8 and also tying the runners (note **5**) at these pins. Continue work, sewing on the inside edge and crossing coarse threads (note **15**) where indicated. It will be necessary to sew twice into some of the holes (in lieu of back stitches) to keep the work level. Sew out in the normal way (note **23**).

The main stem
The main stem should be worked next, starting at the bottom and adding one pair at the central hole on the straight cut edge and also at the other corner hole. Tie the runners at this hole. Hang in pairs for the flower stem on the way up (note **21**). Sew out into the flower. Work the flower stem after laying in a coarse pair (note **22**) and sew out into the flower.

The leaf sprays
The sprays of three leaves are made as in pattern 1, except that the stem is sewn out according to note **23**. The leaf that joins the flower stem is worked normally until it meets the stem. When the runner pair has worked through the coarse thread it is not twisted but is sewn into the stem. The edge pair on that side is sewn into the same hole, tied three times and laid back to be cut off later. The runners continue working and are sewn into each hole of the stem, and the braid is sewn out into the main stem. The filling is a fragment of No Pin (filling 4).

PATTERN 6: HORSESHOE

The horseshoe shape
Set up at 1 (note **1a**) with eight pairs and a coarse pair. Work to hole 2 and add one pair (note **2a**). After making up the edge * work back through the coarse pair and one more pair, then leave the runners and take the last pair they worked through as new runners to hole 3. Add two pairs here before making up the edge and tie the runners (note **5**) when working back. Repeat from * until

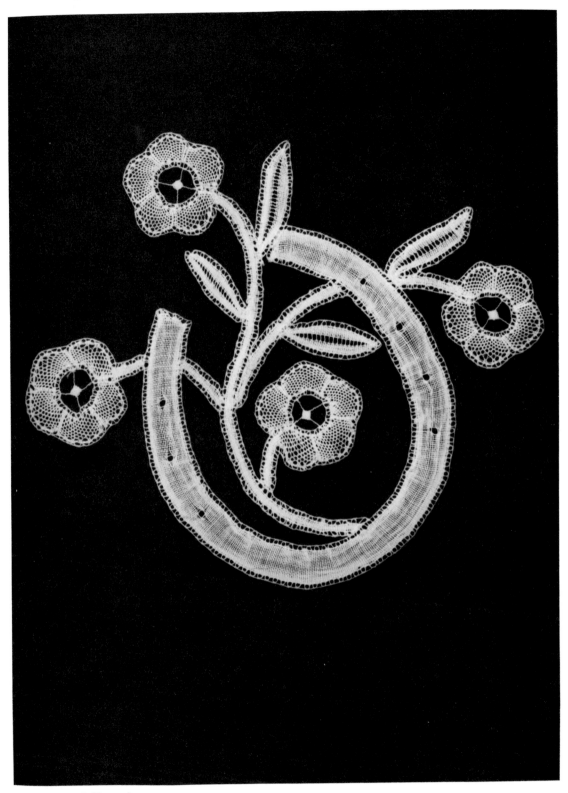

Pattern 6: Horseshoe

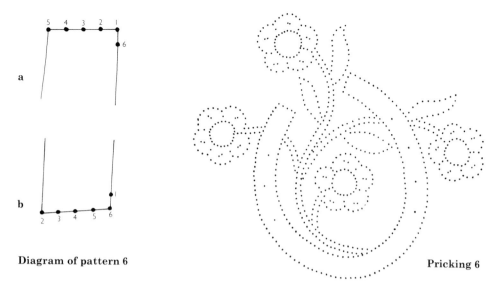

Diagram of pattern 6   Pricking 6

hole 5 has been worked. After tying the runners here, work across all down-rights to the right, set pin 6 and add another pair. Continue in whole stitch to the first of the nail holes, back stitching (note **4**) where necessary. To make the holes, divide the downrights in half, work to the middle and twist the runners three times. Put the pin under the runners into the central hole, then complete the row. Before returning, twist the downright pair on each side of the pin three times. Work to the centre again, twist the runners three times and complete the row.

Finishing

Take out and cut off one pair each side before hole 1 is reached and make a back stitch at hole 1. Cut off two pairs at each side (the four bobbins inside each of the coarse threads). Work to hole 2. Make the edge stitch, work back through the coarse pair, tie the runners once to keep the point up against the pin and work through two more pairs. Leave the runners, and take the last pair they worked through as new runners to 3. Make the edge stitch. Take the two bobbins inside the coarse thread, tie them three times and cut them off. * Work the runners through three pairs, leave them and use the last pair they passed through as new runners to work to 4. Make the edge stitch, take the two bobbins inside the coarse thread, tie them three times and lay them back (do not cut them off). Repeat from * for hole 5, laying back another pair. Work across all downrights to 1, and make up the back stitch. Work to hole 6, add the pin and make up the edge. Refer to note **24**; the two pairs which were laid back at 4 and 5 are used to tie back the bunch of threads.

The flowers

The stems and flowers (10 pairs) are worked as in patterns 2 and 4. The centres of the flowers are filled with a single leadwork using two pairs, which are twisted four times before and after the leadwork is made.

4 ⌗ Flat Honiton Patterns

PATTERN 7: ROSE STEM WITH DIVIDED LEAVES

The stem
Begin at the bottom of the stem with six pairs and a coarse pair (note **1a**). Hang in one more pair (note **2a**) at the hole before the other point, and tie the runners at each hole on the straight cut edge of the stem (note **5**). Work up to the beginning of the thorn. Back stitches (note **4**) will be necessary on the side opposite to the thorn to allow this to be worked. Add a new pair at hole 1, work back to the other side and either back stitch or make up a back stitch. After making up the edge hole at 2 work through the coarse pair, tie the runners and work through two more pairs. Leave the runners and take the last pair they worked through as new runners to 3, and make up the edge there. Take the two bobbins inside the coarse thread, tie them three times and cut them off.

The leaves
Continue working up the stem, taking out pairs (note **3a**) where the stem narrows and adding pairs where it widens into the leaf, which is worked according to instructions for leaf **1**, Chapter 8. The two leaves below this are worked similarly, they can both be completed before the threads are cut off. Begin by sewing three pairs into each of holes 1 and 2 (second diagram), see note **20c**, and add in a coarse pair (note **22**). When the first leaf has been worked, the remaining threads are carried over the stem according to note **16**, but in this case there are only two pairs (the edge pair and the runner pair) to be sewn before the threads are bunched. Complete the second leaf, and sew out (note **23**) into the stem.

The rose
The rose is worked next. Hang six pairs and a coarse pair at 1 (note **1b**), and work first towards 2, adding another pair (note **2b**) at this hole, and at 4 tying the runners (note **5**) at both of these holes. Continue the flower as in previous patterns, laying in two pairs at each of five holes above the calyx (note **21**). Sew out in the usual way, referring to note **20f** before sewing into hole 1. Work the calyx and stem after adding a coarse pair (note **22**).

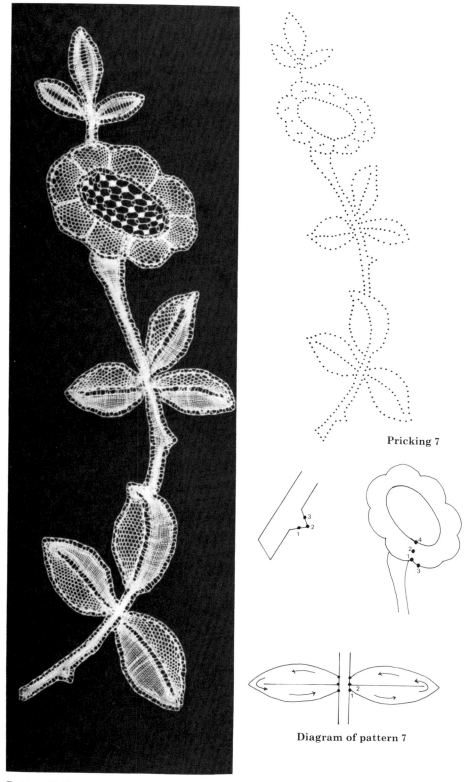

Pricking 7

Diagram of pattern 7

Pattern 7: Rose stem with Divided Leaves

The leaves

The three leaves which join into the stem can also be worked in one piece, beginning with the half stitch section of the top leaf and crossing the pairs from this leaf as previously into the half stitch section of the left-hand leaf. The spray of three leaves at the top of the flower is worked in whole stitch with a twisted vein in the middle. The filling used is Swing and a Pin (filling **11**).

PATTERN 8: OAK LEAVES AND ACORN

The leaves and stem

Set up (note **1a**) at the bottom of the stem with six pairs and a coarse pair; add two more pairs at the first two holes on the right (the outer side of the curve – note **2a**). Work up the stem and into the leaf, beginning to back stitch at the first hole forming the vein of the leaf and at each subsequent hole on this side until the first line of 'windows' is reached. On the outer side new pairs are added as the leaf widens until there are thirteen pairs in all. Work the windows (note **12**).

Continue to back stitch at each hole on the vein side and also cut out one pair on this side where the braid narrows between the lines of windows. As soon as the leaf begins to widen again add pairs on the outer side, one at each hole until there are sixteen pairs. Just before working the second line of windows, cut out one pair on the vein side. After the second line of windows, cut out one pair at each side as the pattern narrows, and immediately it widens again add two more pairs on the outside. On the vein side cut out one more pair before the last line of windows is reached.

This continual taking out on one side and adding on the other is made necessary by the curve of the pattern and the unusual number of back stitches on the vein side, which tends to cause the work to thicken on that side. Reduce to ten pairs for the start of the narrow top part of the leaf and take out two more pairs on the vein side just before the point is reached. The leaf is turned

Pattern 8: Oak Leaves and Acorn

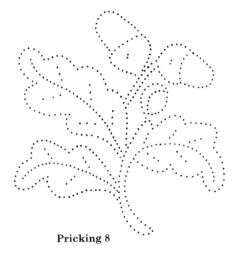

Pricking 8

according to instructions for leaf **1**, Chapter 8. The second side is worked similarly to the first. At the end, cross the remaining threads over the stem (note **16**), and then work the top half of the next leaf.

The acorn

Set up at the centre hole at the top of the acorn which ends in a stem sewn into the leaf, with eight pairs and the coarse pair. Add one pair at each hole on each side until there are fifteen pairs in all. Remember to tie the runners (note **5**) at each hole across the top of the acorn. Work to two holes before the crossing of the coarse threads which divide the acorn from the cup and add one pair on each side. After the coarse thread has been crossed, remember to tie the runners at the hole immediately following on each side. The cup is worked in half stitch with these seventeen pairs. Where the work begins to narrow take out (note **3b**) one pair on each hole until seven pairs are left for the whole stitch stem.

PATTERN 9: BELL

The bell

Set up (note **1a**) at 1 with six pairs and a coarse pair and increase to fourteen pairs (note **2a**), hanging these in on the outer side of the curve. Work round the whole stitch section. After setting pin 2, * hang in a new pair (note **21**) and lay it to one side to be used when working the half stitch section at the bottom of the bell. After making up the edge stitch, take the two bobbins inside the coarse thread and lay them aside with the new pair. Repeat from * for holes 3, 4 and 5. On the other side, cut out one or two pairs as the pattern narrows and the work thickens. Arrange the working so that pin 6 is worked before pin 7, back stitching if necessary. Between holes 6 and 7 only five pairs should remain in the braid. When hole 7 has been worked, the pairs which were laid aside and the new pairs should be brought to the front to lie to the right of the remaining

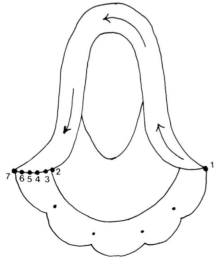

Diagram of pattern 9

Pricking 9

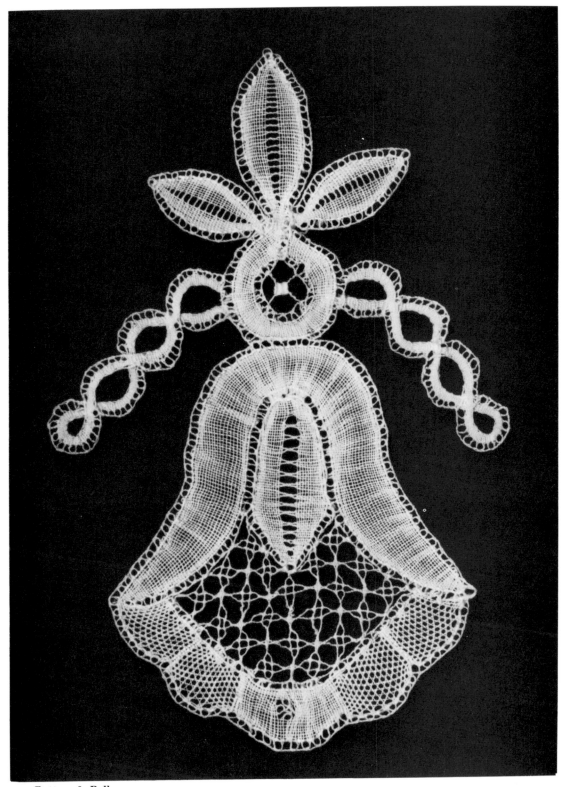

Pattern 9: Bell

five pairs. Untwist the inner edge pair, take the coarse bobbin lying next to it and weave it over and under through this pair and all pairs on the right, except the last. This pair should be twisted three times. With the runners from 7, work one row of whole stitch, make the edge on the inner side and change to half stitch, tie in the runners at this hole to keep the coarse pair in position. Add one more pair. Finish the section with these fourteen pairs and sew out into the start (note **23**).

The whole stitch middle section with the ladder trail is begun at the point with eight pairs and a coarse pair, adding new pairs on both sides until there are nineteen pairs in all. The ladder trail (leaf **7**, Chapter 8) is begun when four pins have been set (including the top pin). After the last hole on each side has been worked, make another crossing of the ladder trail, and when the runners on each side have worked out to the edge, they are sewn into the hole of the curved outer section which is nearest to the last pin. The edge pairs on both sides are also sewn into these holes, tied three times and laid back, to be cut off later. From now on the runners on each side are sewn (without twist either before or after the sewing) on each side and where the section narrows the number of pairs is gradually reduced to twelve. Close the ladder trail near the bottom and sew out the remaining twelve pairs into the last four holes across the bottom. After tying the pairs, cut them off without the usual bunching.

The leaves

The central leaf above the bell is worked next and it runs into the whole stitch ring in the same way as in the second and fourth patterns, the stem runs into the flower. Where the ring touches the bell, the edge pair on that side is sewn out, tied and put aside to be cut off later, and the runners make the usual sewings at that edge. After the runners have been sewn for the last time, sew in a new pair into the hole nearest to the next pin hole to be worked, to become the edge pair, and twist it three times.

The ribbons

The ribbon work on each side of the bell consists of a rib (note **18**) – seven pairs – which crosses back on itself to be sewn into the ring again. Where the rib crosses, the side on which the pin holes are made changes, so that the holes are always on the outside of the curve. After working the pin hole where the rib crosses, twist the outer pair on the plain edge twice more to become an edge pair. Work the runners to this side, twist them three times, set the next pin under them and work an edge stitch and three twists with the new edge pair. The other side now becomes the plain side. The crossing of one rib over another is explained in note **19** (filling 3).

PATTERN 10: CROSS

The outer shape

Set up (note **1a**) with six pairs and a coarse pair at 1 at the base of the cross and add (note **2a**) one new pair at 2 and one at 4. Tie the runners at 2 (note **5**). Work towards the point, taking out one pair at 5 on the inside and adding a new pair on the outside at 6, so as to allow the braid to lie flat around the point. Back stitching will be necessary on the inner side to get round the point. As soon as this point has been turned, begin back stitching on the outer side. Work the other two points like this and add a new pair at 7 and at 8. Remember to tie the runners at every inner and outer point. All the straight pieces are worked

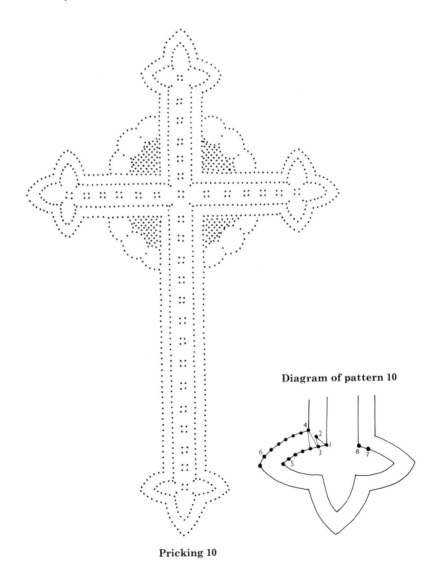

Diagram of pattern 10

Pricking 10

with eleven pairs and the ends of the arms as above. Sew ten pairs into the holes above the half stitch section (note **20c**) and thread a coarse pair through (note **22**). Work the half stitch section, which has purls (note **9**) on the outside, back stitching on the inner side and crossing the coarse thread (note **15**) where indicated.

The fillings

The filling is Trolly Net (filling **15**). The middle of the cross is filled with Four Pin with Half Stitch Bars (filling **25**) and a fragment of Diamond (filling **1**) at the points and centre of the cross.

Pattern 10: Cross

Pattern 11: Leaves and Bud Handkerchief Corner

PATTERN 11: LEAVES AND BUD HANDKERCHIEF CORNER

The leaves and bud

The corner is worked with purls along the entire outside edge (note **9**). Start at the tip of the small leaf on one side of the corner and work up into the top centre leaf of the three. These three leaves can be worked according to instructions for leaf **1** (Chapter 8), and the pairs pass from one leaf to the other without having to be cut off (note **16**). The four pin bud is described in note **11**. Work the spray of leaves on the other side similarly, joining the two centre leaves where they meet (note **20e**).

The stem and fillings

Sew in pairs (note **20c**) for the stem and lay in a coarse pair (note **22**). Work up the stem and around the bud, crossing over into the second stem and sew out (note **23**). The centre filling is Four Pin (filling **6**), the bud is filled with Swing and a Stitch (filling **14**). The two small fillings at the sides are Pin and a Stitch (filling **12**) and small fragments of Trolly Net (filling **15**) fill the space under the bud.

Pricking 11

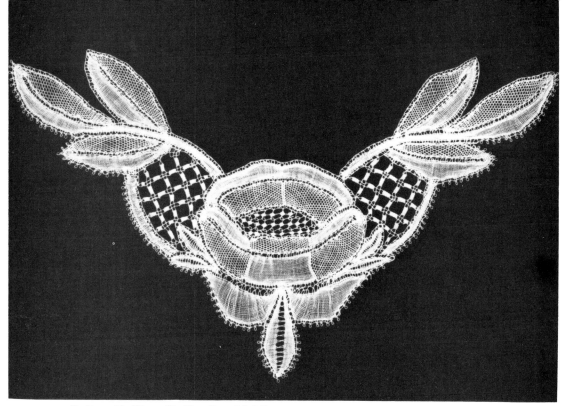

Pattern 12: Waterlily Handkerchief Corner

PATTERN 12: WATERLILY HANDKERCHIEF CORNER

The petals

Start at the tip of the base petal of the waterlily and work half stitch and whole stitch sections alternately, with the coarse threads crossed between them. The turn into the upper of the two base petals is worked as the turn in leaf **1** (Chapter 8). This petal too is worked with whole stitch and half stitch alternating. Just before the section is sewn off into the first petal, two pairs are laid in at each hole above the start of the inner top petal, which is worked next in half stitch. Near the end of this petal, before turning, it is necessary to sew into one or two of the holes of the upper base petal, so that the braid being worked begins to swing round into position to begin the turn described in note **30a**. The topmost petal is worked in whole stitch and sewn off.

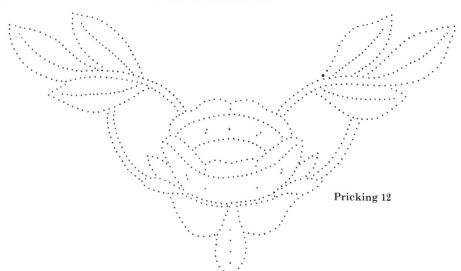

Pricking 12

The leaves

The two small leaves at the base of the lily should be worked next and followed by the sprays of three leaves. Note that the middle leaf of the centre spray begins with a purl (note **27**). The leaves on each side of this need to be carefully worked. They are started at the end nearest the small leaves and many back stitches must be made on the inside, to enable the braid to swing round and finish at the base of the lily. This results in the work thickening on the inside, and therefore threads must be taken out here and added on the outside.

The fillings

The lily is filled with Swing and a Pin (filling **11**) and the spaces on each side with Diamond (filling **1**).

PATTERN 13: ROYAL EDGING

This edging offers few difficulties. Four lengths may be joined to each other along the sloping edge of the edging, to form a square suitable for bordering a handkerchief. The filling is Trolly Net (filling **15**).

PATTERN 14: SCROLL EDGING

This edging is a little more complicated than it appears, as sewings have to be made both before and after the braid has crossed over itself. The sections are worked in whole stitch and half stitch alternating, and the small circles are filled with leadworks.

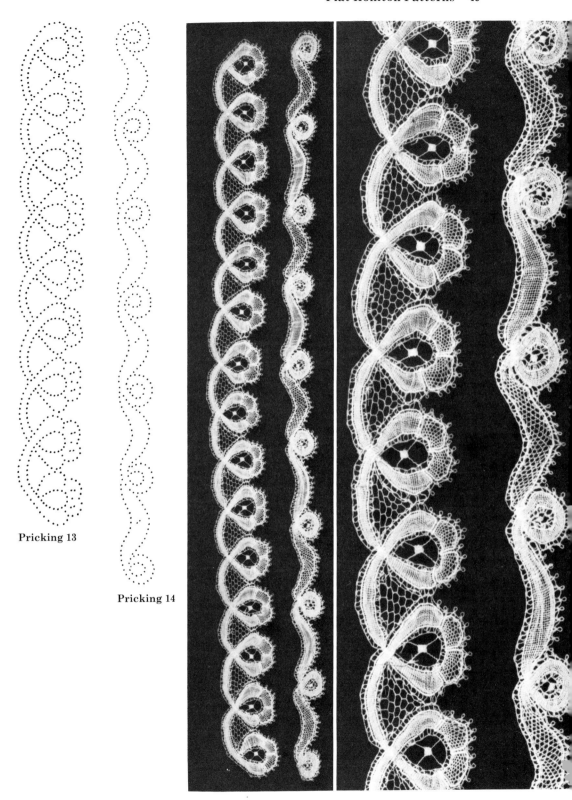

Pricking 13

Pricking 14

Pattern 13: Royal Edging (left)
and Pattern 14: Scroll Edging (right)

Detail of Pattern 13: Royal Edging (left)
and Pattern 14: Scroll Edging (right)

Pricking 15   (a)

Pricking 16   (a)

Pricking 17

PATTERN 15: EXE EDGING AND CORNER

This is intended to be mounted on net for items such as wedding veils. The working is quite straightforward. The filling is Devonshire Cutwork (filling **26**). A corner pricking has been given and one flower of the worked sample fits into this and therefore does not have purls, which are made only along the outer edge of the lace.

PATTERN 16: CULM EDGING AND CORNER

The long centre scroll is worked first and the end is finished according to note **24**. The side scrolls sew off into this scroll. The convolvulus flowers are worked as the ones in pattern **20**. The fillings are Whole Stitch Block (filling **22**) and Four Pin and Leadwork (filling **23**).

PATTERN 17: BRUNSWICK EDGING

This is similar to the Exe Edging but is made in two pieces which are joined by the flower and bar. When working the side leaves on the spray of leaves, start at the tip of the leaf farthest from the scroll, cross over the rib and work the second leaf, which is sewn out into the scroll. The end of the scroll is worked according to note **24**. The fillings shown are **23** and **7**, but when working a long length of this type of edging, it is customary to use a variety of fillings.

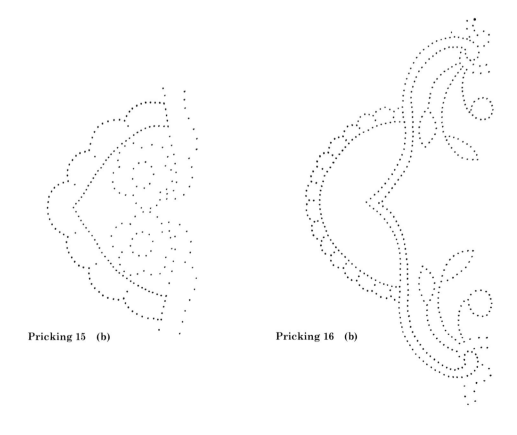

Pricking 15 (b)   Pricking 16 (b)

Pattern 15: Exe Edging (left), Pattern 16: Culm Edging (centre) and Pattern 17: Brunswick Edging (right)

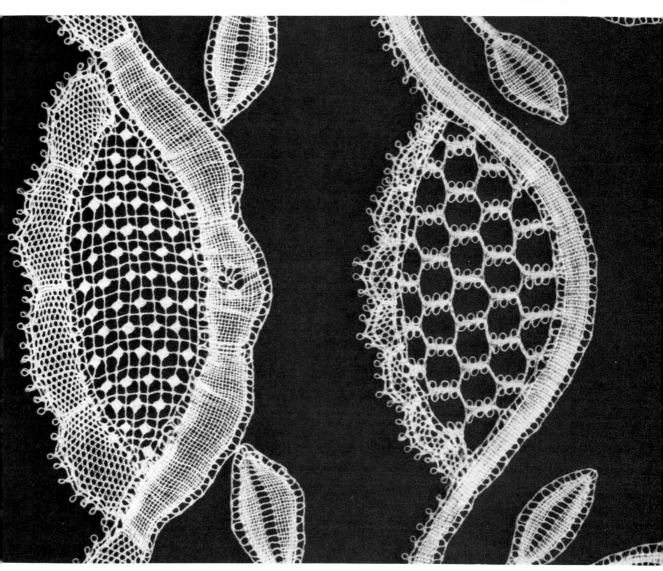

Detail of Pattern 15: Exe Edging (left) and Pattern 16: Culm Edging (right)

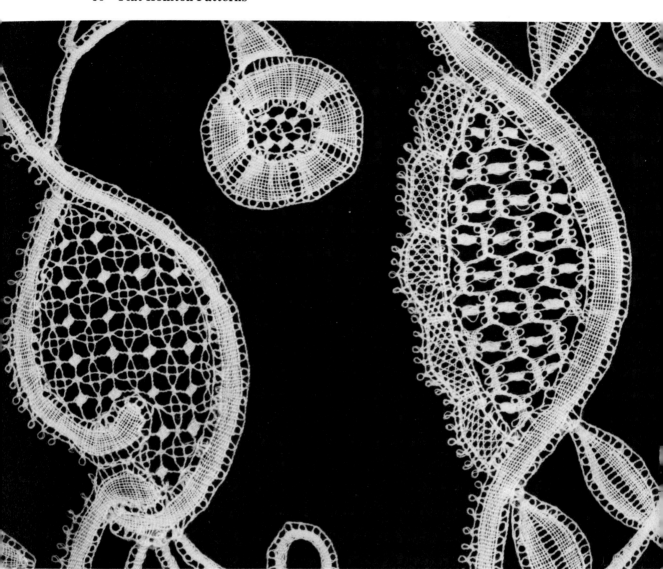

Detail of Pattern 16: Culm Edging (left) and Pattern 17: Brunswick Edging (right)

Detail of Pattern 16: Culm Edging (left) and Pattern 17: Brunswick Edging (right)

Pricking 18

PATTERN 18: BOW

Set up at A with six pairs and a coarse pair and work in whole stitch up the first part of the knot, back stitching on the inner side of the curve, so as to enable the braid to swing round to finish at D. Reduce the number of pairs where the braid narrows. At B lay aside the two bobbins inside the coarse thread to become the inner edge pairs for the top of the ribbon bow. Make a back stitch at C, laying aside another pair. When the back stitch has been made at C, work to D through the few remaining pairs, which are now in position to work the top part of the bow. Weave the inner coarse thread at C through the pair laid aside at C to lie in position at B. Work the top part of the bow. Where this joins into the knot again, turn into the ribbon section just before B, according to note **30b**. This is sewn out into the first ribbon.

The lower part of this side of the bow is worked next, the pairs being sewn into the first ribbon and sewn out into the knot. Work the second part of the knot, setting up at E and working in whole stitch to F, where the pairs are sewn out but not cut off. They are brought into position to make the ribbon end, which finishes at A, where it is sewn out. Set up again half-way down the second part of the knot to work the lower section of the top ribbon, which turns (note **30a**) to work into the second ribbon end. Complete the other parts of the bow. The filling is Four Pin with Half Stitch Bars (filling **25**). This is an example of a filling which must be pricked free-hand, in order to fit into a curved space.

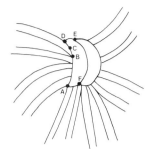

Diagram of pattern 18

Pattern 18: Bow

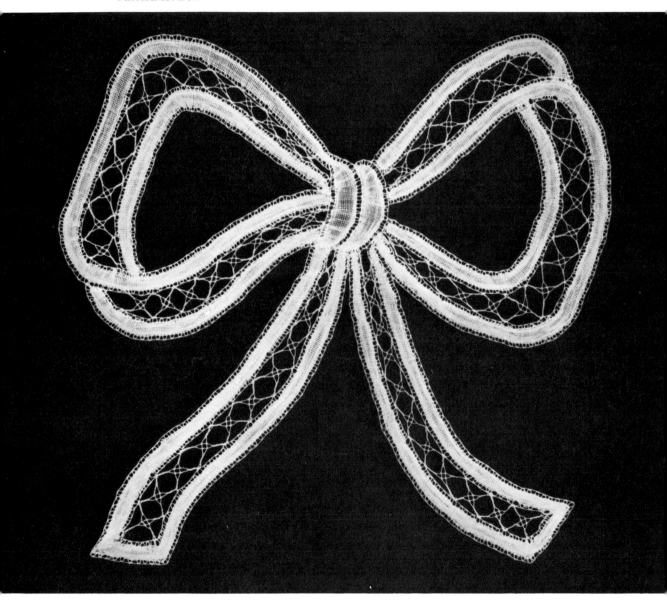

Pattern 19: Butterfly with Trolly Net

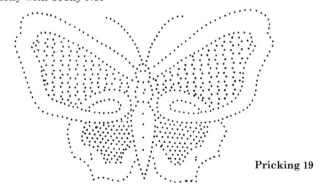

Pricking 19

PATTERN 19: BUTTERFLY WITH TROLLY NET

The body

Work the antennae with six pairs in each. After the last hole make a whole stitch with two edge pairs to join the two sets. Twist the outer pair on the plain side of each feeler (to be edge pairs) and carry one of the runner pairs from the middle through to the end of the row. Weave a coarse pair through all the down-rights (note **22**) and continue to work the head. The eyes are worked according to note **13**, and two pairs are taken out at the end of the head before the coarse thread is crossed. There is a ladder trail vein (see leaf **7**) down the centre of the abdomen and the braid is finished as in note **24**.

The wings

Pairs are sewn in for the wings at the sides of the head. As the top of the wing widens near the first corner, add a pair at every other hole on the outside, whilst on the inside of the corner, where back stitching thickens the texture, take two pairs out. At the points on the lower wing, add a pair on the outside, immediately the point has been worked. The filling in the top wing is Straight Pin (filling **21**), and in the lower wing Trolly Net (filling **15**).

PATTERN 20: CONVOLVULUS PANEL

Upper half

The backward facing flower is worked first. Start at A with seven pairs and a coarse pair and increase where the section widens to twenty to twenty-two pairs by the time B is reached. When the edge at B has been worked, tie the runners (note **5**) and continue to the inner edge, where several back stitches will be necessary. On returning to the outer edge take out two pairs next to the coarse thread at this hole and each of the next two outer holes. Continue to throw out one pair at each hole on this side.

When about half the holes along this outer side between B and C have been used, the work on the inside should have arrived at C, where a back stitch is made, and this is not made up until the turn has been made into the next section. After opening the back stitch at C, work to the outer edge again and work the next edge hole. * Work back through three pairs, leave the runners and use the last pair they passed through as new runners to work to the outer edge and make the next edge hole. Take the two bobbins inside the coarse thread, tie them three times and cut them out. Repeat from * until hole D has been made up. There should be about eight pairs left by this time. Do not take out any more pairs after making the edge stitch at D, but work through to C and make up the back stitch there. Now work to E, and before making up the edge stitch, hang in one pair, which is laid inside the coarse thread, and after making up the edge stitch, hang in another pair which is laid back. Work through three pairs, leave the runners and use the last pair they worked through as new runners to work to the outer edge. Hang in two new pairs before making up the edge stitch. Bring the pair that was laid back at E down to fill the gap below E. Work the runners from the outside through all downrights, as far as the pair brought down from E and one pair more.

** Leave the runners and work to the edge again with the last pair they passed through. Hang in two more pairs. Work to the inner side as far as the runners left in the last row and one pair more. Repeat from ** until the coarse pair on the inside has been worked. Untwist the edge pair on the inside, work the runners through this pair and tie it once to keep the runners up in position. Use the tied pair as runners to work to the outside, where one pair is added. Before working back, tie the old runners (left on the far side of the inner coarse thread) three times and lay them back. Work the runners from the outside through all pairs and sew them at the hole below C. Continue hanging

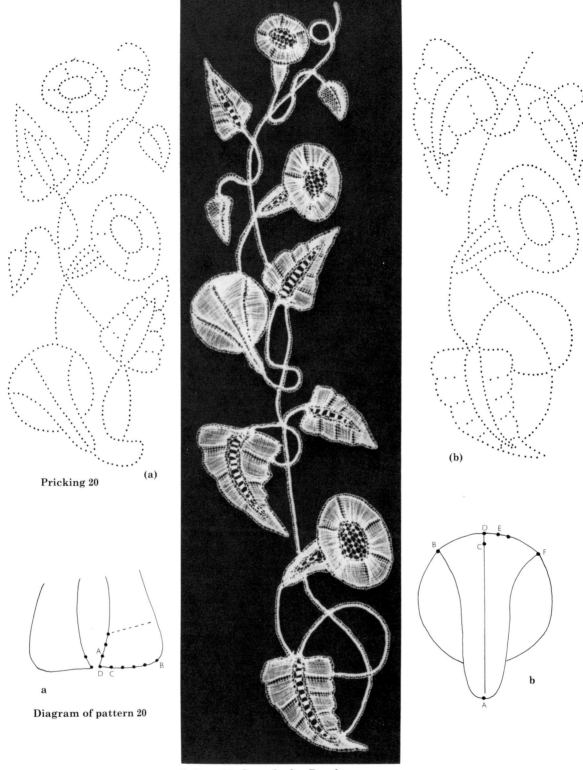

Pricking 20   (a)

(b)

a

Diagram of pattern 20

b

Pattern 20: Convolvulus Panel

in pairs on the outer edge (by the time F has been reached, there should be twenty to twenty-two pairs) and sewing on the inner side. Tie the runners at F and begin to reduce the pairs on that side. The braid is sewn out into the beginning at A. Pairs to work the side sections are sewn into B and one hole below on one side and similarly on the other and these sections are sewn out at the bottom.

The leaf

The leaf which joins to this flower is worked next. Begin at the point with six pairs and a coarse pair and add a pair at each hole on each side. Where the leaf divides work according to note **17**. The cloth work for this leaf should be kept fairly thin, otherwise the windows will not show up well. In this pattern the rows of weaving must be allowed to slant, so that the vein of windows will be on a slanting line when worked. Windows are described in note **12**.

The base of the leaf

Make a back stitch at A and work to B. After making up this pin hole, work through the coarse pair, tie the runners and work through two more pairs. *** Leave the runners and, using the last pair they passed through as new runners, work to the outer edge and make up the next pin hole. Take the two bobbins inside the coarse thread, tie them three times and cut them off. Work through three pairs and repeat from *** until hole C has been made up. Tie and take out a pair here and then work to A to make up the back stitch. Work to D and leave after working this pin hole, laying the pairs aside.

Work down the other side of the leaf similarly. Join the two sets of threads by working a whole stitch with the two adjacent edge pairs. Cut out all coarse threads. Work the runner pair from the right set through to the left, set up the first pin of the ribbed stem and make the edge stitch. Gradually reduce the number of pairs in the rib to seven pairs, and tie each pair that is taken out three times before cutting off. Where this stem crosses the main stem, the side on which the pin holes are made is changed from left to right and the stem is sewn out into the flower. The midrib of the leaf is filled with a row of swing leadworks.

The flower and calyx

For the next flower, set up with eight pairs and a coarse pair at the outer pin hole which marks a line of windows. Choose the line which is just past the calyx, so that when the flower is almost finished it has worked around to where pairs can be hung in ready to work the calyx. Hang in pairs at each of the holes across the centre and possibly one or two on the outer edge, but keep the texture fairly open in order for the windows to show up well.

All the flowers and leaves are worked similarly, except the two small leaves near the top, which are worked as leaf **1** (Chapter 8). The filling in the flowers is Swing and a Pin (filling **11**). The pattern is more conveniently worked in two pieces, which are joined by the main stem.

PATTERN 21: CONVOLVULUS SPRAY

This pattern also looks attractive as two separate sprays. The two leaves at the lower end of the photograph do not appear in this position on the pricking. They were added to make the pattern balance and are in fact taken from the upper part of the pattern.

The flowers with windows and all the larger leaves are worked as in pattern **20**. The two flowers at the centre of the design are a little different. The larger of these has a central ring which is worked first, and begun in a position so that when sewn out, the pairs can be carried on to work the outer part of the flower. When the pairs have been sewn out into the start, the outer ones may be laid in position to begin the outer braid; the pairs on the inner side of the central ring are laid across the braid and sewn into some of the outer holes above where the outer braid starts. This flower is filled with Pin and a Stitch (filling **12**).

The smaller flower consists of a rib which is started around the centre and continued in two scalloped rows around the inner circle. To join the inner circle, after the last hole has been worked, take the runners to the plain side and sew them into the starting hole (note **20f**), together with the edge pair on the pin hole side. Continue by working the first hole of the next section of rib with these pairs. To join into the ring, bring the runners through from the pin hole side, sew them into the circle and work straight back again to the pin hole side. The filling is No Pin (filling **4**), and the filling in the two lower flowers is Blossom (filling **8**), and in the two upper flowers, Swing and a Pin (filling **11**).

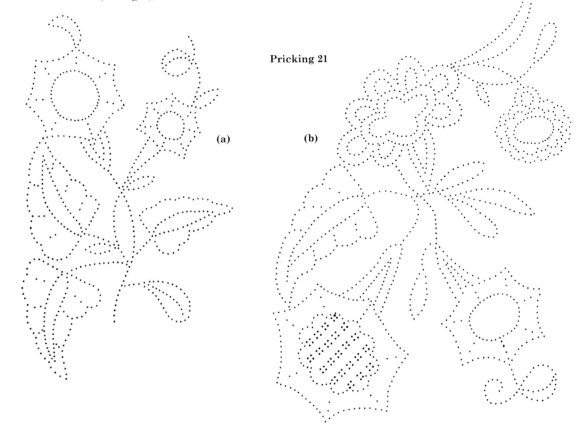

Pricking 21

(a)   (b)

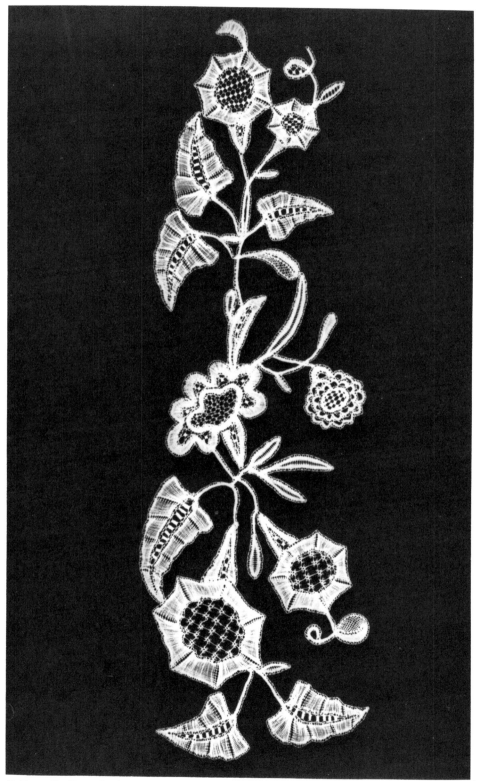

Pattern 21: Convolvulus Spray

PATTERN 22: FISH

The head

Set up with six pairs and a coarse pair in each of A and B. With each set work first towards the mouth side. Add pairs on both sides and continue to C, making sure that when this point is reached the holes which have been worked on the outer side are level or slightly back – not in advance of C. Back stitch if necessary. Make up the pin hole at C with the set from one side. Join the two sets by making a whole stitch with the two adjacent edge pairs at C and leave these pairs hanging. Use the runner from the set which was not used to make up C to work right through to the other side and back, including the inner coarse threads in both rows. These should then be cut off. Continue the head and the snatch pin hole (note **14**). Cut out one or two pairs where the lower jaw curves into the gills.

The body

Before setting pin D, lay aside one pair from inside the coarse thread, set the pin and add another pair, laying it out beside the first. Make up pin D, lay aside another pair from inside the coarse thread. * Work through three pairs, leave the runners and with the last pair they worked through as new runners, work to E and make up the edge stitch. Take the two bobbins inside the coarse thread, tie them three times and lay them out beside those that are already out. Repeat from * for hole F. At this stage lay out one or two more downright pairs (there is no need to tie these) and then work across the remaining pairs to G, and make up the edge stitch there. Weave the coarse thread from F through all pairs which were laid out except the last pair, which is twisted three times and becomes the edge pair. Continue working upper part of body.

Keep the cloth work fairly thin so that the spots will show up well. These spots are leadworks, which are made at random with the runners and the nearest unworked downright pair, using the leading runner bobbin as weaver. When the leadwork is finished, continue the whole stitch with the weaver again used as one of the runners, but being very careful when working not to pull this thread so tight as to distort the leadwork. Finish the section and work the turn into the lower half of the body according to note **30c**. The fins are worked and sewn into the body, the tail being worked in two halves.

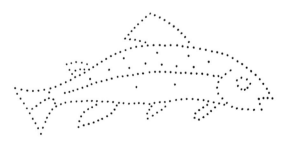

Pricking 22

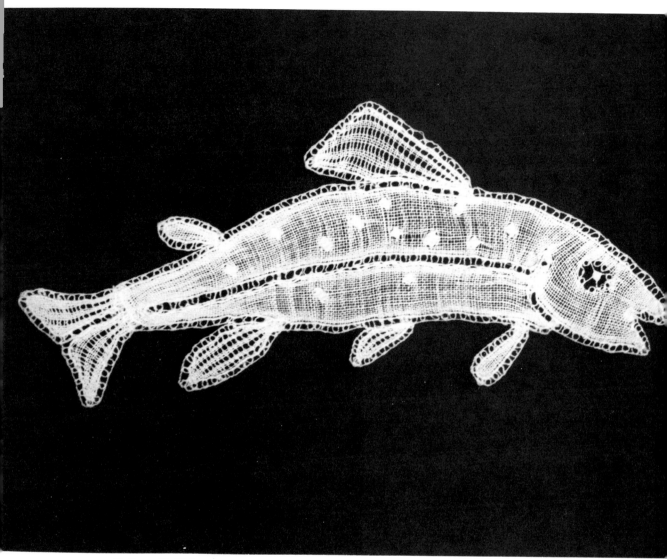

Pattern 22: Fish

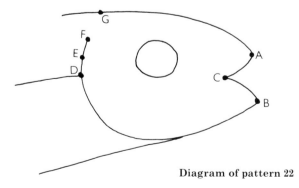

Diagram of pattern 22

Pricking 23

PATTERN 23: PLAIN MAT WITH FILLINGS

This pattern was designed as an exercise in working fillings. Students learned the fillings on one side in class and then worked the second side on their own.

The flowers

The half stitch flowers are worked first, similarly to the rose in pattern **7**. The worked model has purls around the outside. The two trails on each side are worked separately, the second crossing over the first.

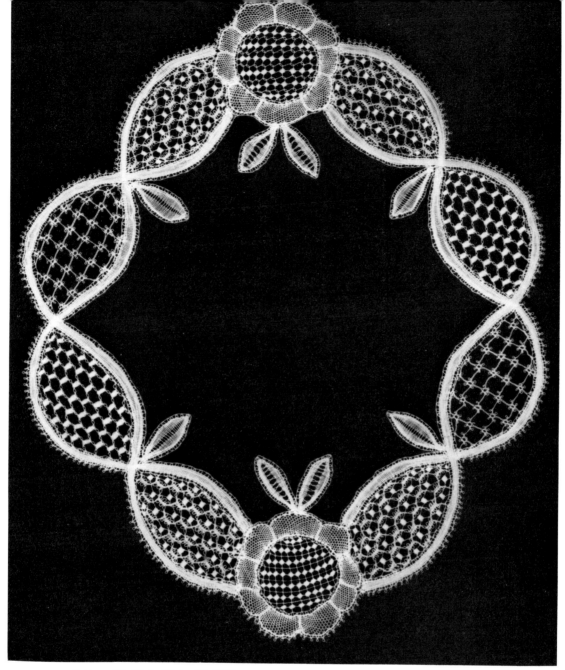

Pattern 23: Plain Mat with Fillings

The fillings

The fillings are Swing and a Pin (filling **11**), Swing and a Stitch (filling **14**) in the flowers, and along the sides Toad in the Hole (filling **9**), which has been used in four spaces each side of the roses in the example illustrated. In the pattern, this has been pricked in only two spaces, to allow students to work another filling of their choice. A number of fillings – such as Italian (filling **10**) – are worked without any pricking. The other two fillings shown are Brick (filling **19**) and Blossom (filling **8**).

5 ⊡ Raised and Rolled Work Patterns

PATTERN 24: MIMOSA SPRAY

The two lowest flowers are worked first and the method of working from the rib round the centre into the half stitch petals is similar to the method described in pattern **5**, Centre Rose and Three-leaf Sprays. Other features occurring in this pattern have been described in other parts of the book. The fillings are Swing and a Stitch (filling **14**) and Swing and a Pin (filling **11**).

Pricking 24

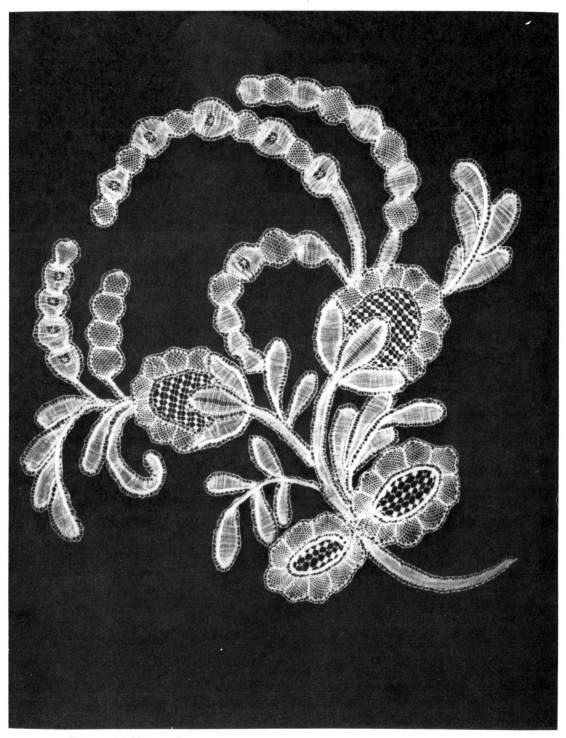

Pattern 24: Mimosa Spray

Pattern 25: Large Flower Spray

PATTERN 25: LARGE FLOWER SPRAY

In both large flowers the centre should be worked first and so it is important to begin at a point where the pairs can be carried on and used in the first outer petal when the centre is finished. The turn between these petals is described in note **30a**. The tops of the petals are sharply rounded and so a great many back stitches will be needed on the inner side (sometimes two in each hole) in order to keep the work level. The second method described in note **4** may also be used, to alternate with the back stitches. The fillings in the lower large flower are Diamond (filling **1**) and Four Pin (filling **6**) and in the upper flower Four Pin with Half Stitch Bars (filling **25**). The centre of the flower is filled with Cartwheel (filling **17**).

(a)

Pricking 25

(b)

PATTERN 26: DAISY FLOWER AND LARGE LEAF

The large leaf

Work the large leaf first. The centre vein is begun at the stem end and works up into the leaf (six pairs and a coarse pair were used and the runners twisted three times in the middle). After the last pin at the top of the vein has been set, lay back the coarse threads and take the runners through all pairs to the other side (including the edge pair). Tie the runners and all other pairs three times, open the runners and tie them round the bunch made of the other threads. Bow off the bobbins but leave the ends of thread long so that they can be held in one hand when sewings are taken here later, when the half stitch part of the leaf is being made. If these threads were to be cut short immediately there would be a danger of the pin holes being lost. The other veins are started at the tip and sewn out into the centre vein. Each segment of the leaf is worked separately, begun at the tip and divided at the top of the vein, each half being worked separately. The pairs are sewn out into the centre vein.

The flowers

The large central flower is started with the whole stitch petal in the middle and the pairs worked into the half stitch petals. The daisy is started with the central rib at a point where the pairs will be in position to work the next rib up one of

Pattern 26:
Daisy Flower and Large Leaf

Pricking 26

the petals, when the central ring is joined. The pairs are worked from one petal to the next as described in the Raised Flower, pattern **43(e)**. The flower next to the large leaf is started at one end of the whole stitch section and at the other end the turn into the half stitch petals is worked as described in pattern **9**: Bell. The bud is started at the base of one of the petals with a rib to the point (see leaf **4**: Simple Raised Leaf). When the petal is complete, the pairs are rolled and ribbed up the other side petal. The middle petal and the calyx are worked afterwards and sewn out into these two petals.

Pattern 27: Raised Butterfly backed with Half Stitch

Pricking 27

PATTERN 27: RAISED BUTTERFLY BACKED WITH HALF STITCH

The body

Work the feelers first, using six pairs for each rib. Set a pin into the hole at the top of the head between the feelers; hang two pairs round it and twist them twice each. Leaving aside the two outer pairs from the rib on one side and one outer pair from the rib on the other, to be the new edge pairs and runners, weave a coarse pair through the remaining bobbins and lay it to the back of the pillow. Leave the first downright bobbin on each side, take the next two threads, tie them three times and cut them out. Work one row and lay the coarse threads into position. The rest of the body is worked as for the Butterfly in pattern **19**.

The wings

The small circles of rib in the middle of the wings are made first, and when these are joined the ribs are carried on and sewn out into the body. Next, sew in seven pairs at the body to work the rib along the leading edge of the wing. The photograph shows clearly how this is changed into braid (a coarse pair is added here). When passing the first division of the wing hang in the seven pairs needed for the rib which is sewn out into the upper circle. Leave the bobbins making the outer edge aside and work this rib. Return to the outer braid and continue working this, hanging in and laying aside two pairs at every inner hole, to work the whole stitch section later. Finally, hang in the seven pairs required for the next rib and again leave the bobbins making the outer braid aside. Work the rib and sew it out into the lower circle.

The whole stitch section of the wing can now be worked, the runners being top sewn at each side. When the circles are reached, a number of pairs will be sewn out into them. The section is sewn out into the body. Return to the outer braid and work this until the next division of the wing is reached. Hang in seven pairs here and then lay aside the bobbins of the outer braid and work the rib, which is sewn out into the body. Continue the outer braid, hanging in two pairs at every hole on the inside and at the lower corner cut out the coarse threads and change to rib again to work the lower edge.

The lower whole stitch section with twisted veins is worked next and the pairs sewn out into the body. Work the Diamond fillings. When the pairs which have worked this filling are sewn out and the bobbins cut off, the ends of threads should not be trimmed short until after the half stitch backing has been worked, otherwise the ends of the threads from the filling could easily become loose and pull away. The half stitch backings are worked next and the pairs for these are sewn into the braid at the outer edge. Several pairs are sewn out at the tops of the rings and some are hung in again where needed below the rings.

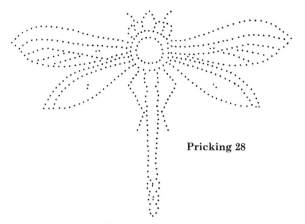

Pricking 28

PATTERN 28: DRAGONFLY

The body

The body is started at the tail end. The middle section of the abdomen is rows of windows (note **12**), with two or three rows of whole stitch at both ends. The abdomen works up into the ring of the thorax and is sewn out at the beginning of the ring. The head is started at the top and sewn out into the ring and a narrow rib forming the eyes is sewn in at the head and out at the ring. The front feet are joined to the eyes by one or two sewings and the side on which the pin holes are worked is changed here. Sew out into the ring.

The wings

Begin the front wing at the outer tip and work the front edge first. After the first two or three holes of whole stitch, open the ladder trail (see leaf **7**). In this case, the crossing of the runners alternates with a leadwork made with the runner pairs (one twist before and after the leadwork). The turn into the half stitch section is worked according to note **30a**. At the point where the first whole stitch tap starts (just before the half stitch section is sewn out into the wing tip), hang in three pairs at each of two holes to work the first tap later. The taps at the lower edge of the wing are worked next using the six pairs which were hung in and adding one or two more pairs. The taps are worked as described in leaf **5**: Raised Leaf with Taps.

    The back wing is started like the front wing. After the turn, work the rib along the lower edge and fill in with half stitch.

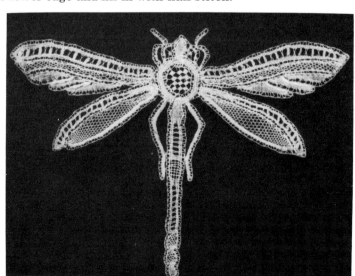

Pattern 28:
Dragonfly

PATTERN 29: PEACOCK

The legs

Start with one of the feet, setting up with seven pairs (no coarse pair) at A and working a whole stitch braid to B. After setting the pin and working the edge, take the runners through all pairs (including the edge pair on the other side) and tie them twice. Tie all the other pairs twice and lay them between the tied runners and tie them twice over the bunch. Make a short roll, winding the runners round all the other threads and sew this pair in at C. Now work the rib up the leg and along the inner side of the thigh, where several pairs must be hung in and laid aside to work the whole stitch later. Continue the rib to the upper point of the thigh and down along the outer edge, again laying in a few pairs along the curve near the end. At the last few holes, lay out a pair from the rib. Sew out the runners on one side and the edge pair on the other where the

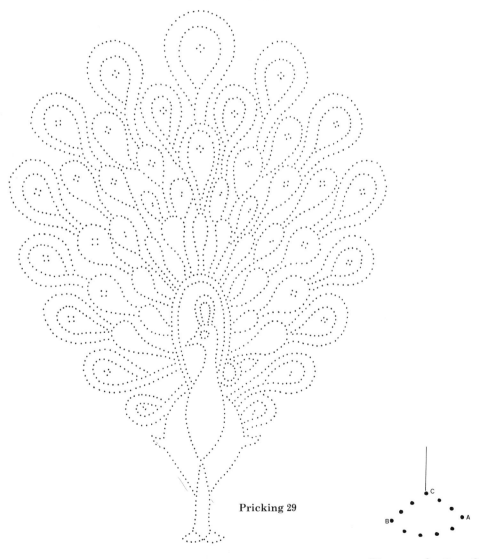

Pricking 29

Diagram of pattern 29

thigh joins the leg, tie the sewn pairs, turn the pillow and use these pairs to work the whole stitch, bringing in the pairs which were laid aside as they are needed. Sew out into the rib at the top of the thigh.

The head

The head is begun at the beak end and sewn out into the thighs. The eye is a snatch pin hole with leadwork (note **14**).

The tail

The inner tail feathers are normal raised pieces. For the large tail feathers on the outside, the outer braid is worked first, and the pairs for the inner part are laid in on the inside of the top curve for working later.

Pattern 29: Peacock

PATTERN 30: POPPY AND HAREBELL SPRAY

This pattern requires very little explanation. The harebells have a ribbed stem which works up into the middle petal which is worked like the Simple Raised Leaf (leaf **4**). The pairs are then rolled up the inside of one of the side petals, going into a rib for the tip and worked back, crossed to the other side petal where they are again rolled up the inner side as before. The sprigs of leaves are also raised on one side. The filling is Swing and a Pin (filling **11**).

Pattern 30: Poppy and Harebell Spray

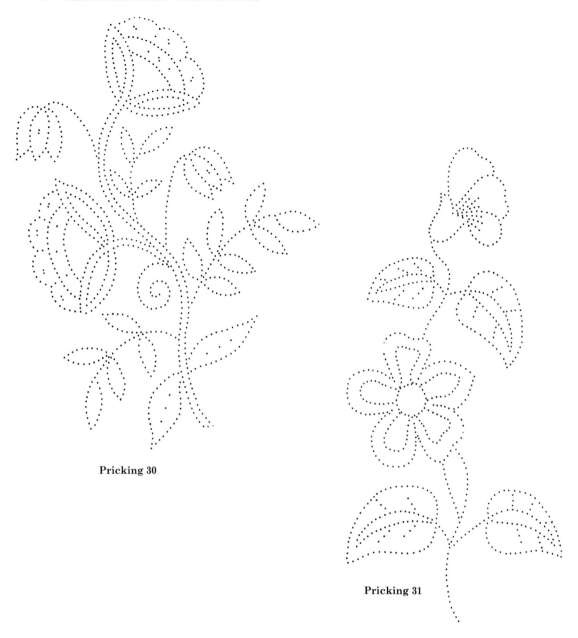

Pricking 30

Pricking 31

PATTERN 31: PERIWINKLE SPRAY

The flower and leaves

The central flower has a ribbed ring in the middle which works into the petals as in the daisy in pattern **26**. The turn between petals is worked according to note **30a**. The central space has No Pin (filling **4**) and the petals are filled with Pin and a Stitch (filling **12**). The leaves are worked like those in the Convolvulus Panel (pattern **20**).

Pattern 31: Periwinkle Spray

The bud

The rib for the calyx of the bud is started at the centre top and worked right round the calyx. No pairs are hung in for the clothwork as this will later be done with the pairs which have been used for petals. When the calyx rib has been joined, the pairs are used to rib up the centre petal. Leave this rib before any pairs for the clothwork have been hung in. Sew in seven pairs into the calyx and rib up the side of the smallest petal. Put these pairs aside before any pairs for the clothwork have been hung in and complete the centre petal, working the rib and hanging in pairs across the top. Put aside pairs out of the rib at the last two or three holes and then work the whole stitch, sewing the runners on both sides. At the bottom of the petal any pairs still left are laid aside for later use on the calyx.

The rib for the smallest petal is completed next, pairs being laid in around the top as usual and these make the clothwork, after the rib has been sewn out into the calyx. The pairs that are left at the end of this petal are also laid aside for the calyx. The pairs for the rib of the other petal are sewn into the top of the calyx and the rib made on the other side of the petal. This is worked as the centre petal and the pairs at the end are sewn into the rib of the calyx and used with the others to work the clothwork. Sew out and tie at the base of the calyx but do not bunch the pairs.

PATTERN 32: CRESCENT MOTIF WITH FLOWER AND TAP LEAVES

The photograph shows clearly where the rib circle for the centre of the flower begins, so that when the circle is joined the pairs can be carried on into the petal (see the Daisy in pattern **26**). The turn between petals is described in note **30a**. When the last petal has been made the pairs turn and work a braid into the tap leaf (see leaf **6**). The pairs for the braid making the stem into the second tap leaf are sewn in at the centre circle of the flower. The fillings in the flower are Swing and a Pin (filling **11**) and Trolly Net (filling **15**) and the large spaces are filled with Four Pin (filling **6**).

Pricking 32

Pattern 32: Crescent Motif with Flower and Tap Leaves

PATTERN 33: EMBLEMS

Daffodil

Start with the trumpet. The rib is begun at one side and the inner side of the ring is worked first, turning into the outer side. After joining into the start of the ring, the rib is worked down one side of the trumpet and pairs are laid in all around the base for the subsequent clothwork. Sew out the rib into the ring, sewing the edge pair on one side and the runners on the other, cutting out two pairs and tying the remaining three pairs before bunching and cutting off. Do not trim off the ends until the trumpet is complete. Fill in with whole stitch. Sew out the pairs into the inner side of the ring, cutting off those not required for the filling, which is Swing and a Pin (filling **11**).

The centre petal is made first, the pairs for the rib being sewn into the base of the trumpet. The transition from one petal to the next is described in the Raised Flower, pattern **43e**. The three petals on one side are made first and finished off, then the pairs needed to work the rib for the first petal on the other side are sewn into the side of the centre petal.

Shamrock

The rib for the shamrock stem is started by sewing the pairs into two holes of the daffodil petal. The rib works up the side of the first leaflet of the shamrock. Pairs are hung in at each hole near the top and two pairs are hung in at each hole across the top. When the top of the first lip has been passed, work back and forward across some of the laid-in pairs to fill in the lip and still hang in pairs, two or even three at each new pin hole; these may not all be needed but it is better to have them ready, rather than having to sew more in. Any that are not required can easily be taken out. When the pin hole in the dip between the two lips has been reached and two pairs hung in * work back through two pairs and leave the runners. Use the last pair the runners worked through as new runners to work to the next pin hole in the second lip. Hang in two pairs here and also one which is laid to the back of the pillow to fill any gap which may develop here. Repeat from * but hanging in only two pairs at the next pin (omitting the pair which is laid to the back). Bring the pair which was laid back down into position in the gap at the second hole from the dip and work the runners across the whole width of the leaflet. More pairs will have to be hung in at the pin holes on the left and pairs which were hung is on the right are gradually brought in. The great number of pairs needed for the top of the leaflet has to be reduced quite quickly as the section narrows. The method used to work the second lip of each leaflet is similar to that in leaf **4**: Rib, Leadwork Centre and Points. Seven pairs should remain at the base of the first leaflet and these make the rib for the centre leaflet.

Rose

This has a ribbed ring in the middle and the method of working out into the petals is described in pattern **5**: Rose and Three-leaf Spray. After sewing out

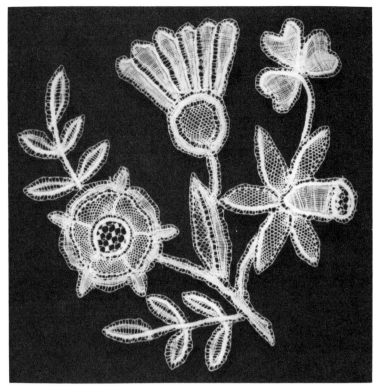

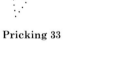

Pricking 33

Pattern 33: Emblems

the half stitch section, one of the points of the sepals is worked from the tip, adding pairs on each side and tying the runners well. Sew out into the half stitch section and then bring some of the sewn-out pairs (nearest to the part to be worked) round to work the first section of the whole stitch outer circle. These pairs should include one of the coarse threads, which is used on the outer side only, together with an odd bobbin to be its partner. Leave the bobbins just before the next sepal is reached. Set up and work the next point, sewing out and bringing the bobbins round as before to use for the next whole stitch section. Complete the first whole stitch section and sew it into the sepal just made. The main stem is worked next starting at the base, the method of dividing the braid being described in note **17**.

Thistle

This cannot be worked until the Divided Leaf (see leaf **1**) has been completed, and the pairs for the thistle stem may be hung in and put aside while the leaf is being worked. The braid of the stem works into the ring round the calyx and pairs are hung in and laid aside across the top for the half stitch filling, which is worked after the braid forming the ring has been sewn out. The first section at the top of the thistle is ribbed, the turn from one section to the next being worked as in the daffodil petals and subsequent sections being rolled to the top. The sprays of leaves are raised on one side.

PATTERN 34: FUCHSIA

The leaves
Begin by working the small plain leaf with a twisted vein above the two upper flowers. This is worked down the main stem and into the first half of the large central leaf. This is similar to the convolvulus leaf, having veins made by slanting lines of windows. Put aside the bobbins when the first half of the leaf has been worked.

The flowers
Hang seven pairs into the plain leaf to work the rib for the stem of the flower that overlaps the large leaf. The rib works right round the knob of the calyx and is joined to itself. The pairs from the rib will be sufficient to work the whole stitch filling in the centre and they can subsequently be used to rib up the large petal. On the way up, pairs can be hung in and laid aside to be used later to work the rib of the petal which overlaps the leaf.

Sew out the pairs of the large petal into the calyx and then work the petal for which the pairs were hung in. When this is finished, the pairs from it can be rolled into position to begin the rib for the first section of the 'underskirt' of the blossom. The other sections are rolled and the turn from one to the next is described in pattern **43(e)** – Raised Flower. The smaller backward facing petals are also ribbed. The stamens (see the diagram) are begun with five pairs at A. Rib to B, making the pin holes facing the flower. Rib to C, where one pair is hung in and laid aside. Rib to D. After setting the pin, work the runners through to the plain side, tie them twice, put all other rib pairs between them and tie them twice again over the bunch. Roll the tied pairs once or twice round the bunch to reach back to C, where all the bobbins are laid between the bobbins of the pair which was laid in and put aside here, and this is tied twice over them. Rib up to the flower with these six pairs and sew out. All flowers are worked similarly.

The large leaf and reversing leaves
Return to the pairs left at the point of the large leaf and work the second half. Where the flower petal overlaps, sew out the edge pair and a few downrights and cut these off. The outer coarse thread is laid aside and brought in again later on the other side of the petal, where a few downrights and an edge pair are again sewn in. The unworked part of the coarse thread which crosses over the petal is cut off later.

At the end of the leaf the remaining pairs are attached to the base of the first half and turned (note **30b**) to rib up the small leaflet, which is worked next and the pairs crossed over to work the first part of the reversing leaf. This part is completed first and the pairs sewn out into the stem. The central rib for the reversed part of the leaf is started at the top and is sewn out into the first cloth stitch section. Three or four of these pairs can be used for the half stitch side, the remainder being cut out. A few more pairs are needed for the half stitch and

Pattern 34: Fuchsia

Pricking 34

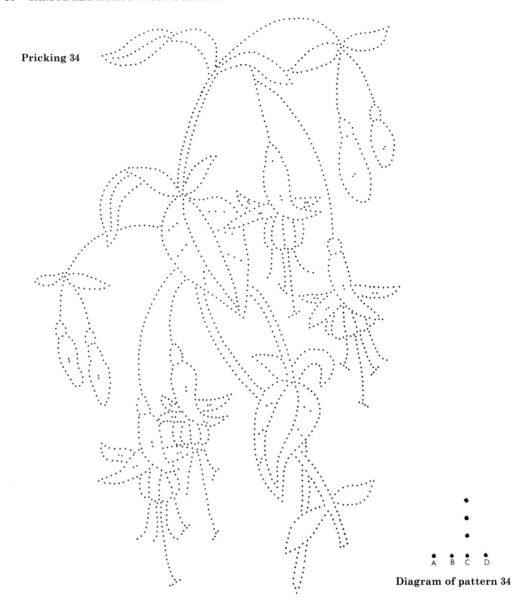

Diagram of pattern 34

these are sewn into the side of the whole stitch section. Only a very few pairs are needed to turn around the top of the rib, where several sewings will be made into the starting hole.

The other side is worked in whole stitch and sewn out at the base. The rib for the other reversing leaf is started at the top, being worked right down to the stem. The side on which the pin holes are made changes at the crossover. The rib pairs are sewn into the stem and turned to work the lower whole stitch part of the leaf. Cross over the rib at the half-way point and work the half stitch section next, turning round the tip of the leaf and finishing with the narrow whole stitch segment. The leaves are filled with Pin and a Stitch (filling **12**).

PATTERN 35: JAPONICA

The top flower

To work the top flower, rib around the centre, starting and finishing at a hole from which the threads can be used to rib up the side of the petals. Add pairs at the top holes and use with the rib pairs to work half stitch down to the centre circle. Work as described in note **30a** across the base of the petal, reducing to seven pairs. These are used to roll up the side of the petal just made and then continue in rib across the top of the next petal. Lay in pairs at each hole of the rib to work this petal in half stitch as before, and repeat for the remaining petals. The last petal is worked down to the centre, the pairs are sewn into the centre rib, tied and cut off separately (not bunched).

The bottom flower

To work the bottom flower, set up seven pairs at 1 and use them to rib round centre petal A. At holes 2, 3, 4 and 5 add one pair and lay aside to use later for half stitch filling. Complete rib and join at 1. Use these seven pairs to rib round petal B. Lay in one pair at each of five holes after the first and lay aside to use later for half stitch filling. Sew this rib to the rib of petal A and reduce to four pairs; turn and rib round centre along base of petals C and D. Sew to rib of petal A, turn, make up to seven pairs and rib round petal E. Sew off into petal A and use these pairs with the pairs laid in and put aside when working petal

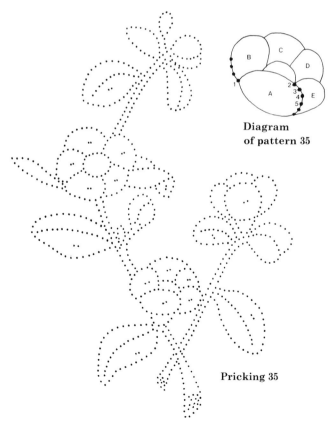

Pattern 35: Japonica

Diagram
of pattern 35

Pricking 35

A to fill this petal with half stitch. The pairs remaining at the end of this petal can be carried forward to be used with the five pairs laid aside on petal B to work half stitch across all remaining petals. The two top petals have no rib at the top. Work two rows of whole stitch to divide these two petals as there is no coarse thread to weave across. Sew the downrights here and there to the rib holes as half stitch crosses over them. Sew off, but do not bunch.

The stem and leaves

The base of the stem is worked from the point in whole stitch and has three rows of holes made by twisting the runners. Lay in pairs on one side near the end of this little cut section, to be used in working the main stem. The turning from the cut section into the main stem is similar to the method used in the Bell (pattern **9**). Most of the other stems work up into buds or leaves, which are Divided Leaves (see leaf **1**) except where they have been raised. To work the turned leaf attached to the flower, sew seven pairs into the flower and rib up side of the first section; at the top two holes lay in five pairs to use later for the top turned section. Complete the first section as leaf **4**. Sew off into flower but do not bunch. With the five pairs put aside rib and work the top turned section as in leaf **4**, Chapter 8. Sew off into the first section, tie and cut off. The other small part is worked in the same way, sewings being taken into the rib and also to the side of the first section. Sew off.

PATTERN 36: WILD ROSE AND FORGET-ME-NOTS

Large flowers

To make the large flowers, rib round petal A, starting at 1, join to the beginning and use the pairs to rib up the outer side of the turned section of petal B2. Turn at the top and fill in the turned section with whole stitch. Work into and fill petal A with half stitch; reduce to seven pairs and rib up the inner side of the turned section of petal C3. Turn at the top and fill turned section with whole stitch. Reduce to seven pairs, work rib round the centre of the flower 4, and sew off.

Sew six pairs at the base of petal B at 5, use them to make a roll up the side of the completed turned section, add one pair and rib round this petal, adding pairs at each hole along the top and putting these aside to use later for the filling in. Complete the rib round the petal and sew to the rib enclosing the centre of the flower. Use these pairs to make a roll up the rib just worked to the point at which petals B and D separate, and leave the pairs here. Fill petal B with half stitch. All these pairs are sewn into the centre rib, tied and cut off separately (not bunched).

Return to the pair which made the roll and continue working petals D, E and C as described above, except that having ribbed round the top of petal C, use six of the rib pairs to make a roll along the completed turned section and sew off at the base. Fill the petal with half stitch. The filling is Swing and a Pin (filling **11**).

Pricking 36

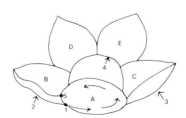

Diagram of pattern 36

Pattern 36: Wild Rose and Forget-me-nots

Stems and leaves

Work stems and sepals after the main stem and large rose leaf sprays have been worked. These are the Divided Leaf (leaf **1**). When working up the first section of these leaves, work the points at the side as the bottom of the convolvulus leaves in pattern **20**, i.e. tie runners at the point, work back through two more pairs, * leave the runners and with the last pair they passed through used as runners, work back to the next hole at the point and make up edge stitch. Tie two bobbins inside the coarse thread three times and cut off. Work back through three pairs and repeat from * until all holes at the point are made up. Remember to back stitch on the inside to keep the work level.

After the top of the leaf has been turned, the small points at the side are worked as described in pattern **37**. The small leaves below have an outer rib and are filled with whole stitch. After the first leaf, the threads cross the stem and are used to work the second leaf. Sew off.

The bud

To work the small bud, work the stem in whole stitch (no coarse threads) and into the calyx. Add pairs each side and tie back well (note **5**). Back stitch on the last hole before the bud and work to the last hole on the opposite side, then work as in note **30a**. Use seven pairs to rib outside of one section of the bud and fill with half stitch. Roll seven pairs up the side of this completed part, and fill the next section with whole stitch. Sew off into calyx. The sepals are worked with rib and whole stitch. Work the larger bud as the small bud until the rib along the outside of the first petal has been made; reduce to six pairs and rib one of the small tips. Add one pair and fill with whole stitch. Take one pair out and rib and fill the other tip. Use these threads to work in whole stitch down the first petal. Sew off at the bottom of this section. Sew seven pairs into the calyx to rib and work opposite section. The centre of this bud is worked in half stitch.

PATTERN 37: CORNFLOWER

The leaves and buds

The ferns in this pattern are worked as described in leaf **6**, Raised Leaf with Taps, except that here the main vein consists of a whole stitch braid and not a rib. The cloth stitch circles below the central cornflower have a ribbed centre. The buds below the lowest flower are made of small taps.

The flowers

The cornflower has a ribbed ring at the centre, which is started in such a position that when it has been completed and joined, the pairs can be used to rib up the side of the first petal next to the calyx.

Pricking 37

Diagram of pattern 37

Batsford Book Information Service

NAME _____

ADDRESS _____

_____

_____

POST CODE _____

Please fill in your **NAME** and **ADDRESS** together with the TITLE of this book if you wish to receive further information on **Batsford** books. (If you have sent us a card already, please pass this on to a friend).

TITLE OF BOOK _____

 **B.T. BATSFORD LTD**
4 Fitzhardinge Street, London W1H 0AH

Do not affix Postage Stamps if posted in
Gt Britain, Channel Islands, N Ireland
or the Isle of Man

Postage
will be paid
by licensee

Business reply service
License no: WD240

**B T Batsford
4 Fitzhardinge Street
LONDON
W1E 1YZ**

Pattern 37: Cornflower

At hole A lay aside one pair from the rib. Work to hole B. After setting this pin, tie the runners when they have passed through the first downright pair and continue working the tied runners to A, where they work through the pair which was laid aside here. Tie this pair once and use it as new runners to work to C. Make the edge here and work to A again, where the runners are sewn into the lower side bar of the pin hole. Work to hole D and hang in two pairs here before making the edge.

Work back through three pairs, leave the runners and take the last pair they passed through as new runners to work to E. Hang in two new pairs here before making the edge – the first being laid inside the first downright thread and the second being laid to the back of the pillow. Work through three pairs again, leave the runners and take the last pair they passed through as new runners to F. After making the edge here, tie the runners after the first downright pair, before working them to E, where they work the pair which was laid to the back. This pair is tied and taken as new runners to G, where the edge is made. Work to hole D and sew the runners here, then work to H.

Now work back across all pairs to A, where the runners are sewn once more. Work to J, where two more pairs are added. The last point is worked similarly to the previous point and the runners are taken across the whole width of the petal when the pin hole on the outer side, level with or just above the level of J has been completed. The sprays of small flowers are ribbed, rather like the ribbed flower in pattern **21**: Convolvulus Spray. The cornflowers are filled with No Pin (filling **4**).

Pattern 38: Primrose Spray

Pricking 38

PATTERN 38: PRIMROSE SPRAY

The leaves

Work the full leaf first. The open vein is worked as described in leaf **3** – Rib, Leadworks Centre and Points – but in this case the side veins are made at the same time. Try to arrange the leadworks so that there is no need to make them where the side veins join. The side veins are made like those in Leaf with Raised Veins (leaf **5**). In this case the two pairs must be hung in each time a side vein is worked and taken out again when it is finished.

When there is only one hole of the vein left, cut out one downright pair from each rib. Work the runners from the side opposite to that on which the last hole is towards the last hole and make a back stitch here. Now work to the bottom hole on the outside of the leaf. Hang a coarse thread on a pin above the leaf and lay it in position as the outer downright thread on the cloth stitch side. Take out a thread to make an even number of bobbins. Turn the other bobbins and work up the cloth stitch side of the leaf. Use top sewings on the vein side. Work four pin buds (note **11**). When passing the side veins attach the runner as described in Leaf with Raised Veins (leaf **5**). Work round the top of the leaf and down the other side, changing to half stitch. Sew out at the base. The other leaf is worked as above, sewing out into the first leaf.

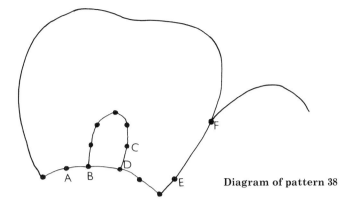

Diagram of pattern 38

Primrose centre ring and stamens

Hang seven pairs round a pin in hole A. Work one hole of rib, and before making up the edge stitch at B add one pair and lay it inside the first downright thread as usual. Make up the edge stitch. Leave the outside (edge) pair and lift the next four pairs over it and use them to make the rib of the stamen. Remember to tie the runners at the topmost hole of the stamen. After working hole C take the runners back to the plain side.

Open out the first downright pair of the main rib, lift the four pairs which worked the rib of the stamen over the twisted edge pair of the ring and lay them between these two bobbins. Tie these two bobbins twice over the bunch. Tie twice and cut out one pair from the bunch. Continue working the ribbed ring. When it has been joined, use these pairs to rib up the side of the nearest petal. Hang in approximately nineteen pairs across the top (two pairs at each hole in the middle), lay these aside and continue the rib to the bottom of the petal.

After working hole E take the runners to the plain side and sew them and the edge pair on the other side to the next hole of the central ring. Tie the sewn pairs twice, open out one of these pairs, put all but the other sewn pair between these and tie them twice over the bunch. Use them to make a roll to F and the other sewn pair to sew the roll to the edge. Leave these pairs and work the half stitch filling the first petal using the pairs that were laid in. Work to just below the level of the top hole of the stamen.

The pairs are now divided and the half stitch worked in two sections, one each side of the stamen. To join into the stamen, select one of the central downright pairs and sew it into the top hole of the stamen. Tie this pair once. This will be the runners for one side. Bring the runners from the side and sew them also into the top hole. Continue each section, sewing in to the stamens on the inner sides and into the rib at the outer sides. Reduce the number of pairs, sew out the remaining pairs into the ring at the bottom and cut off. The roll at F now continues as a rib and each petal is worked as the first, use the rib pairs to make a short roll to the ring and sew out. Do not trim the ends off short until the half stitch has been completed and sewn out.

PATTERN 39: HONEYSUCKLE

The flowers

This spray is started with the largest flower, which has a half stitch braid centre, working out into the rib of one of the petals. Some of the petals are worked in two parts and the ones with the pointed tops are worked like the points in the Cornflower petals (pattern **37**). In some cases the pairs from one petal can be used to work the next, using the method described in the Raised Flower, pattern **43e**, but some of the petals may have to be sewn out and new ones started again independently. The main stem works right up into the berry, the three sepals at the base of this being raised.

The leaves

The leaves have a ribbed vein and as most of the leaves are opposed, the rib can be started at the top of the vein in one leaf, crossed over to the stem, and worked to the top of the vein in the opposite leaf. After the last pin hole has been

Pattern 39: Honeysuckle

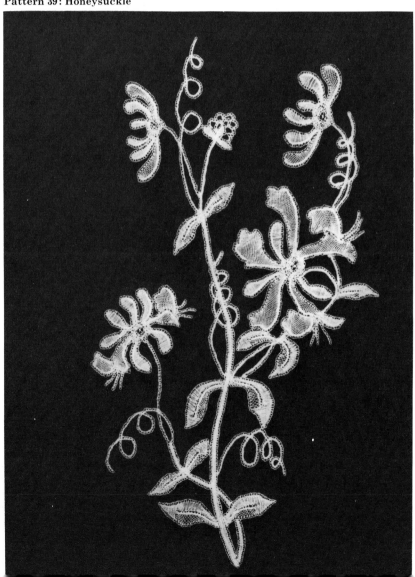

Pricking 39

worked, the runners go through to the plain side and are tied twice. Tie all other pairs twice bunch the bobbins and cross and tie the outer pairs over the bunch. Cut the bobbins off but do not trim the ends of the threads until the sewings have been taken in this top hole. The leaf is then set up at the tip and the threads divided when the top vein hole has been reached. The two halves are then worked separately and the pairs reduced and sewn out into the stem.

Pricking 40

PATTERN 40: MAT WITH SPOTTED NET

The sprays
This is begun with the circle of whole stitch braid surrounding the centre and all the leaf and flower sprays are joined to it. All the components of these sprays have been described elsewhere in this book.

The fillings
The central space is filled with Snatch Bar with Leadworks (filling **5**). The ground round the flower sprays is Spotted Net (filling **16**) and the fillings in the outer spaces are Four Pin (filling **6**), Rib Square and Leadworks (filling **20**), Brick (filling **19**), Italian (filling **10**) and Honeycomb. (Honeycomb has not been described in this book, since it belongs more properly to Point Ground lace and is very rarely used as a Honiton lace filling.)

Pattern 40: Mat with Spotted Net

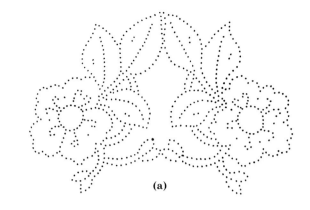

(a)

Pricking 41

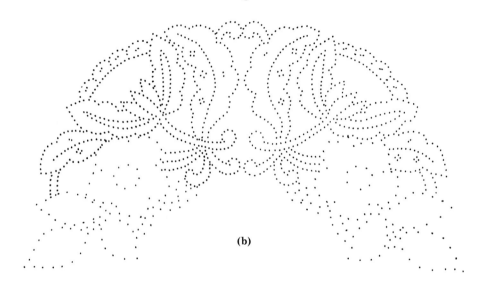

(b)

PATTERN 41: ROSES AND LILIES FLORAL MAT

This is one of four mats which were designed for me by my first teacher, Miss Effie Kemp, and is one of the few designs by this talented lacemaker which have survived.

The roses

The half stitch flower with the raised stamens is begun with the ribbed central ring, which is started at the division between two petals and two holes before the first stamen. Work the rib to the stamen hole end, after making the edge here, leave the outer (edge) pair and lift the next four pairs over it to make the rib of the stamen. Work the rib round the small ring at the top of the stamen and take a sewing to complete the circle. Tie the sewn pair twice, put the other three pairs between the tied pair and tie it twice again over them.

Pattern 41: Roses and Lilies Floral Mat

Make a short roll to the central ring. As this roll is so short it need not be attached to the stamen. Lay these four pairs between the bobbins of the nearest downright pair of the ring rib and tie these twice over the bunch. Continue the ring and stamens and at the end after closing the ring work the pairs up into the half stitch petal as described in pattern **5** – Centre Rose and Three-leaf Sprays. Add a coarse thread and remove one bobbin to make an even number. Work the half stitch petal, attaching the runners here and there to the stamens (sewing with the runner, i.e. the leading thread, and putting the same bobbin through its own loop) and sewing into the central ring. Since there is no coarse thread on the inner side, the outer coarse thread is worked through all the downright pairs and back to its original position between the petals.

The scrolls
The three small scrolls at the base of the large flower are worked next. Start at the base of the stem of the large flower and work a rib around the scroll furthest from the large leaf. Work back in whole stitch, carry the threads on for the rib of the middle scroll. Work back and use the same pairs to rib and work the last scroll.

The lilies
The pairs from the last scroll are used to rib up the stem of the flower and around the centre sepal. The few pairs laid in at the top of this sepal are used later to work a backing of whole stitch with a ladder trail vein (see leaf **7**). The pairs from the rib of the centre sepal are used to rib and work the two side sepals and after the second of these, they work the whole stitch stem, the rib of which has already been worked. The side petals of the large flower have a rib and leadwork vein, similar to the one described in leaf **3**. The half stitch top of the flower follows and some of the pairs from this are turned and used in the narrow whole stitch band with a ladder trail vein.

The leaves
The leaves begin with a rib down the middle, which is started at the top vein hole and worked to the bottom of the leaf, where the pairs turn, work up one side of the leaf, round the top (sewing several times into the top vein hole) and down the other side, where they are either sewn out or work into a stem. The fillings are Pin and a Stitch (filling **12**) and No Pin (filling **4**) in the flowers, and Toad in the Hole (filling **9**), Straight Pin (filling **21**), Four Pin (filling **6**) and Spotted Net (filling **16**) in the surrounding spaces.

PATTERN 42: FLAT BROOCH MOTIFS

(a) Buttercup

This is worked on the same principle as the second pattern but using fewer pairs.

(b) Acorn

The empty acorn cup is worked first in half stitch, referring to notes **1b**, **2b**, **4**, **3b**, **5** and **24** (ten pairs maximum). The stem is hung in at the bottom and sewn out into the cup. The acorn is worked next similarly to the acorn in pattern **8** (Oak Leaves and Acorn). The acorn stem is sewn to the first stem and then turned into the leaf stem – see note **30b** for the method. The leaf is worked according to instructions for leaf **1**, Chapter 8.

(c) Butterfly

The feelers are worked in rib with five pairs each, with the pin holes on the outer sides. Leave each rib after the last pin hole has been worked and the edge stitch made. Before joining the two sets for the body, work the runners of one rib through one downright pair and leave them to become downrights. Weave a coarse pair through all downright pairs and lay it to the back of the pillow until one row has been worked. Work this row and make the edge stitch. Take three downright pairs from different parts of the row (i.e. one from each side and one from the middle). Tie these pairs three times and cut them off. Bring down the coarse threads into position. Work the body in whole stitch. The small spur is worked as the thorn in pattern **7**, Chapter 4, and the braid finished according to note **24**.

To work the large wing, set up with five pairs and work four holes of rib. Give two more twists to the outer pair on the plain side (to become an edge pair). Thread a coarse pair through the downrights. Work the braid adding new pairs at each hole on each side so that there are twelve pairs in all by the time the work is level with the top holes of the snatch pin hole (note **14**). Add four more pairs. The veins at the base of the wing are made by twisting the runners three times in the middle, and two pairs away on each side. The wing is sewn out into the body.

The smaller wing is worked similarly but with fewer pairs below the snatch, reducing to five pairs to obtain a neat finish when sewing out. For the lower wing the pairs are sewn into the larger wing and sewn out into the body.

(d) Poppy

Begin at the stem end, work up into one of the sepals and round into the other sepal after crossing the stem (note **16**). When passing the position where half stitch begins, lay in two pairs (note **21**) at each hole. The sepal is sewn out into the stem. Of the pairs which were laid for the petal, leave two pairs on the inner side and one pair on the outer side to be the edge pairs and runners. Weave a coarse pair through the remainder (note **22**), and work the petals. The filling is Swing and a Pin (filling **11**).

(e) English Rose

Work the centre of the rose as the rose in pattern **7**, using fewer pairs. Sew out the pairs in the normal way and cut off the inner coarse thread. Lay aside the edge pair on the outer side together with the outer coarse thread. Form the remaining bobbins into two bunches, the outer bunch containing seven bobbins and the remainder in the inner bunch. The bobbins in the inner bunch can be cut off.

Take one of the inside pairs of the outer bunch as runners and sew them into the outer edge and use to work through all the pairs including the coarse thread to the first hole on the right towards the point. Add one pair before making the edge stitch with the edge pair which was laid aside. Work back through two pairs, leave the runners and with the last pair they passed through, as new runners, work out to the last hole before the point. Add one pair here. Work to the inner side and sew the runners well back to avoid any gap. Work out to the point and after making the edge stitch here, work back through the coarse pair, tie the runners, and work through two more pairs. Leave the runners and with the last pair they passed through, as new runners, work to the next outer hole.

After making the edge stitch here, take the two bobbins inside the coarse thread, tie them three times and cut them out. One more pair should be cut out on the inside, leaving five pairs to work the outer whole stitch circle. Work the other four points following the instructions given for the thorn in pattern **7**. Take top sewings (note **20b**) on the inner side of the circle as it will be necessary to sew twice into nearly all the holes on that side. The leaves are Divided Leaves (leaf **1**).

PATTERN 43: RAISED BROOCH MOTIFS

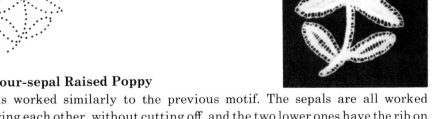

(a) Raised Poppy
The sepals are worked following instructions for the Simple Raised Leaf (leaf **4**). After the first sepal, cross the pairs over the first rib and begin working the rib for the second sepal. The filling is No Pin (filling **4**).

(b) Four-sepal Raised Poppy
This is worked similarly to the previous motif. The sepals are all worked following each other, without cutting off, and the two lower ones have the rib on the lower side. The filling is Swing and a Pin (filling **11**).

(c) Rose Bud

This flower is worked all in one piece. Work the stem first running into one of the raised centre petals, as in Simple Raised Leaf (leaf **4**). Cross over and roll up two holes as in Raised Leaf with Taps (leaf **6**), to bring the pairs into position to work the rib for the second whole stitch petal. When reducing the pairs at the end of this petal, cut off a single bobbin, so that an odd number of threads remain to cross over into one of the outer half stitch petals. Hang a single coarse thread from a pin above the work and lay it into position as the third thread from the outer side. Work the half stitch petal, top sewing twice and sometimes three times into each hole on the inside to keep the work level. (Ten pairs were used for the widest part of the petal in this example, reducing to eight pairs to work the top of this petal.) Cross into the top petal. Before beginning this, tie one pair from the bunch three times and cut one of these bobbins off. Lay in another coarse thread on the inner side, complete this section and cross to the last petal, taking out the inner coarse thread and one other bobbin. The filling is No Pin (filling **4**).

(d) Harebell

Start at the bottom of the stem, work in a rib with seven pairs and the pin holes on the right. On the curve halfway up the stem work back stitches at two holes to allow the rib to lie flat. The calyx is worked with the pin holes on both sides, adding one pair on each side and tying the runners at these two holes. These two pairs are taken out at the last two holes of the calyx and the pairs are now in position to rib up the right side of the centre petal. Hang in two pairs at each of the three top holes of the petal and leave these aside for the half stitch work later.

After working the last hole of the rib, take the runners through to the plain side and sew them into the calyx together with the edge pair on the other side. Roll these pairs up the side of the petal (as in Raised Leaf with Taps, leaf **6**) to where the pin holes of the side petal begin and leave them. Now return to the centre petal and use the six pairs which were laid in to work half stitch, sewing into the rib on both sides.

At the end these pairs are used to roll up the other side of the centre petal. Work rib to point of the side petal, hanging in and laying aside three new pairs at the first three holes, and laying aside a pair from the rib (as in Simple Raised Leaf, leaf **4**) at the next hole.

After turning at the point, work through all pairs including those that were laid aside, except the last. Leave the runner and tie once the last pair they passed through, which will now be used as runners to work to the outside. The remainder of the petal and the four pin bud (note **11**) are worked in the usual manner. The plain leaf should be worked first and the pairs crossed over the stem to work the Divided Leaf (leaf **1**).

(e) Raised Flower

Rib the centre circle with seven pairs beginning and finishing at a hole where they will be in position to rib up the outside of the first petal, hanging in one pair at each hole, starting at 1 and finishing at 2, at each of the two holes before 2, also lay aside one pair out of the rib. Work across in half stitch (remembering that the first and last pairs should always be worked in whole stitch). Towards 1 leave the runners and tie the last pair they worked through once, to hold the runners up tight against the pin hole. The tied pair is used as the new runner pair. Reduce by three pairs before the rib circle is reached.

At hole 3 make a back stitch and work to 4 where the runners are sewn. Work the runners through one pair, tie them once and work them through two more pairs. Leave the runners and with the last pair they passed through as new runners work back to 5 where they are top sewn. Tie three times and cut off the second and third downright bobbins. Work the runners to 3 and make up the backstitch there.

Work to 6 and top sew the runners there. Tie three times and cut off the second and third downright bobbins. Cut out one other downright pair on the right hand side. Tie the sewn runners twice, open them out, lay the remaining six pairs between them and tie the runners over this bunch. Leave out one pair from the bunch and roll the tied runners round the remaining five pairs up to where the holes of the next petal begin. Sew this pair to the hole nearest the first hole of the next petal and tie it twice to hold the roll back. Use the pair left behind to attach the roll (note **20g**).

The other petals are worked similarly. In some of these not all thrown out pairs need to be cut off, one or two can be laid aside and used later for the centre filling (filling **4**, No Pin). This saves having to sew them in. After the filling, these pairs may be used again in the ribs leading up to the whole stitch circles.

6 ⬚ The Sampler

The fillings used in the Sampler are described in Chapter 7, and the leaves in Chapter 8.

The central flower
The Sampler is begun with the middle ring of the large central flower. This is begun at a point where, when the ring is complete, the pairs will be in position to work the first petal. After working the last hole on the outer side of the ring, work the runners back to the inside and sew them, together with the edge pair,

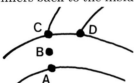

Diagram of the Sampler's central ring

at hole A. Tie them once. Sew one of the central downright pairs at B and the edge pair on the other side at C. Take the two pairs which were sewn at A across to D and sew them in again here to be the new edge pair and runners. Lay all the downright threads into position between C and D, the inner coarse thread being brought across to be the fifth thread from D. The edge pair at C is twisted three times and the half stitch petal is started. The turn between the petals is described in note **30a**.

The scrolls
The large scrolls which are sewn out into the flower are worked next. In the sampler, the first method of starting them, described in note **31**, was used, but the second method may also be used. The smaller scrolls which join into these are worked next and are followed by the buds on each side of the central flower.

The stems
The pairs for the stem are sewn into the flower and the rib stem works right up into the bud. At the last two holes before the rib goes into the little ring at the top of the bud, hang in two pairs at each hole and lay these aside, to fill in the

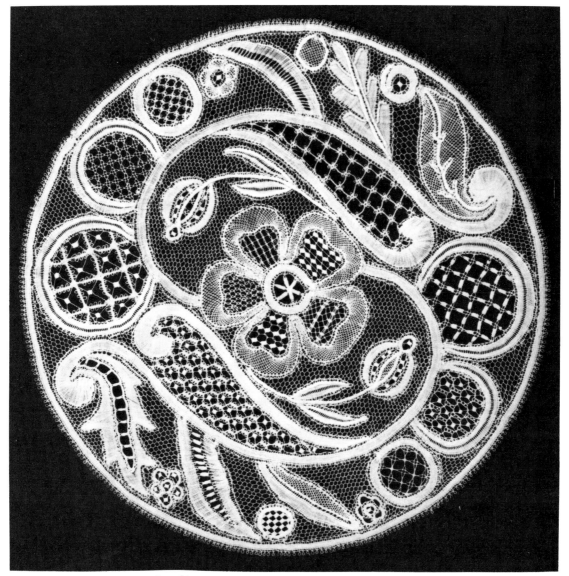

Pattern 44: The Sampler

half stitch centre later. When the little ring is complete and the rib has crossed over itself (note **19**), hang in two more pairs at each of the next two holes and lay these aside with the other four pairs.

The buds

Finish the rib by sewing the runners on one side and the edge pair on the other into two holes of the completed rib at the base of the bud and then use them to work the outer whole stitch section up one side of the bud. Sew out into the ring at the top. Next, work the half stitch down the centre of the bud, using the eight pairs laid aside. It is preferable, when working half stitch along a raised edge to work a whole stitch with the last pair of downrights at each end of the row as if it were a coarse pair. The runners are top sewn (note **20b**) into the rib holes at the end of every row, since there are no edge pairs here.

At the end of the half stitch section, sew the runners into the rib on one side and the outer downright pair into the rib on the other side. Tie both pairs twice and use them to bunch and tie the other pairs. One of these pairs is then top sewn into the rib at the base of the unworked whole stitch section, to become the edge pair on this side. The other bobbins are laid in position and the side section is worked and sewn out into the ring at the top.

Sampler diagram

Key to sampler diagram

Fillings
1 Diamond
2 Toad in the Hole Variation
3 Jubilee
4 No Pin
5 Snatch Bar with Leadworks
6 Four Pin
7 Whole Stitch Block Variation
8 Blossom
9 Toad in the Hole
10 Italian
11 Swing and a Pin
12 Pin and a Stitch
13 Pin and a Chain
14 Swing and a Stitch
15 Trolly Net

Leaves
L1 Divided Leaf
L2 Centre Leadwork and Pin
L3 Rib, Leadwork Centre and Points
L4 Simple Raised Leaf
L5 Leaf with Raised Veins
L6 Raised Leaf with Taps
L7 Ladder Trail

R   Raised circle with half stitch centre

Pricking for
the Sampler

RAISED CIRCLE WITH HALF STITCH CENTRE

Half stitch can be used to fill a small space such as inside a raised circle, although it is not technically a filling. The sampler shows an example (at **R**) of half stitch being used to fill a circle.

The rib is begun anywhere along the circle and pairs are hung in and left aside at the next few holes. The rib is continued to the end, and at the last few holes before the rib joins, pairs are laid in and left aside again. At the last two or three holes a pair can also be laid aside from the rib. The rib is joined by sewing and tying the edge pair on one side and the runners on the other, to the starting hole. Tie and cut out one or two downright pairs from the rib and lay the remainder over the rib circle, together with the pairs which were laid aside. As runners, choose a pair which will work across a number of the other pairs in a straight line without leaving a gap between the rib and the half stitch at the top. Complete the centre of circle and sew out. Do not bunch the threads.

Detail of the Sampler, showing fillings 1 and 2

Detail of the Sampler, showing fillings 3 and 4, and leaf 1

Detail of the Sampler, showing fillings 5 and 9, and leaves 2 and 3

Detail of the Sampler, showing fillings 6 and 7

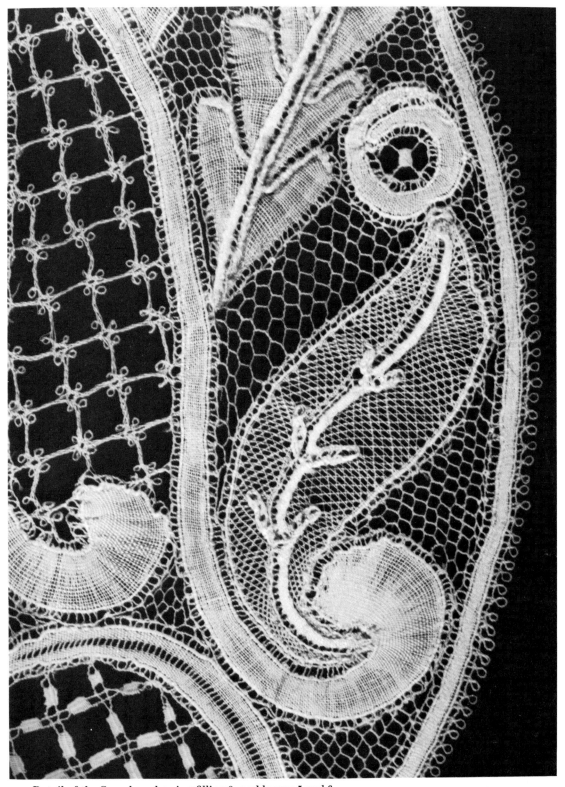

Detail of the Sampler, showing filling 8, and leaves 5 and 6

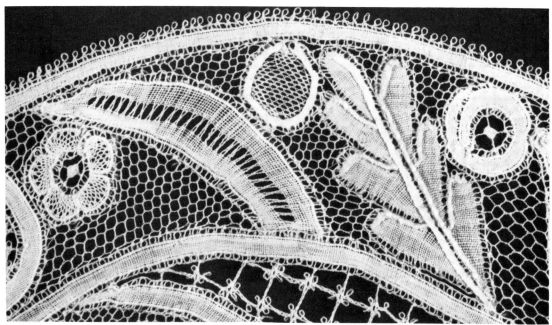

Detail of the Sampler, showing leaves 6 and 7, and the raised circle with half stitch centre

Detail of the Sampler, showing fillings 10, 11, 12, 13 and 14

7 ⬚ Fillings

The great variety of fillings is one of the characteristic features of Honiton lace. Many Honiton lacemakers prick their fillings by eye, without the aid of graph paper, sometimes using a ruler as a guide. This makes it possible to fit a filling into a given shape in such a way that the groups of holes are complete at the edges and matching at both sides. An example of such filling worked into a curved space can be seen in the Bow, pattern **18**. However, to give the student some idea of the size the fillings should be, they are shown here on a grid and should be pricked on *one millimetre graph paper*.

The pairs for the fillings are sewn into the completed braid above and as near as possible to the groups of holes where they will be required, and often more than one pair will need to be sewn into the same hole. When sewing out pairs which have worked a row of filling, they are either tied three times and laid back to be cut off later, or they are brought in again to be used in a subsequent row if they are needed to fill in a widening space.

When a filling has been completed, and all the pairs have been sewn out and tied, the bobbins must be cut off and the ends of the thread trimmed before the pins are removed from the filling. Take out all the pins from the filling.

It often happens that the groups of holes of which many fillings consist are not complete at the edges of the space to be filled. When this happens, work the incomplete group as nearly as possible to the instructions given for these fillings – it is often possible to make a sewing into the edge of the braid to replace any missing holes. This can be clearly seen in Toad in the Hole (filling **9**) in the sampler.

HOW TO PRICK

Transfer the dots for the chosen filling onto tracing paper, lay this over the pricking, and prick through into the space to be filled. Another method is to prick a block of the filling onto a piece of acetate, or used and washed X-ray plate; this is laid over the pricking and pricked through onto the pattern. These pricked 'templates' can be used again and again, providing that the pricking is done carefully, so as not to enlarge the holes in the template.

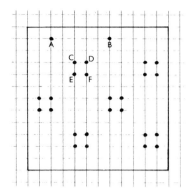

Filling 1: Diamond

FILLING 1: DIAMOND

(See Sampler diagram.) Sew in two pairs above A and two pairs above B. These may be sewn into adjacent pin holes of the completed braid. With the two pairs above A, work a whole stitch and twist both pairs three times. Add pin A between the two pairs. Repeat for hole B.

   With each set of two pairs make a narrow leadwork to reach as far as C and D. When both leadworks are complete, twist all four pairs three times and set pins C and D between each two pairs. With the two centre pairs work a whole stitch (No Pin). Twist both these pairs three times. With the two left-hand pairs work a whole stitch, twist both pairs three times and set pin E between them. With the two right-hand pairs work a whole stitch, twist both pairs three times and set pin F between them. With the two centre pairs work a whole stitch and twist both pairs three times (No Pin). Each two pairs now work another lead-work to the group of holes diagonally below, where they are joined by two pairs coming in from the opposite direction.

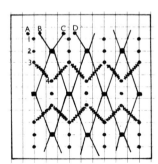

Filling 2: Toad in the Hole Variation

FILLING 2: TOAD IN THE HOLE VARIATION

(See Sampler diagram.) Sew two pairs into each hole A and D. Sew three pairs into each hole B and C. With the two pairs from A work a bar of three half stitches to reach to I. Do the same with the two left-hand pairs from B. With the two middle pairs of these four, work a whole stitch and one twist and set pin I between them. Work a whole stitch and one twist with each two side pairs. Enclose the pin with a whole stitch and twist, using the two middle pairs. Set pin 2; then again work a whole stitch and twist with the two side pairs. Enclose the pin with the two middle pairs, making a whole stitch and twist. Set pin 3 and work another whole stitch and twist with each two side pairs. Enclose the pin with a whole stitch and twist.

Work a bar of three half stitches with each two pairs and leave. Work another block of three holes as above, using the two pairs from D and the two right-hand pairs from C.

Twist the two pairs remaining at B and C five times each and make a square leadwork with them, twisting them five times again after the leadwork. Work the left-hand pair of the leadwork in whole stitch through the two nearest pairs coming from 3. Leave the leadwork pair aside and with the two pairs from 3 work a bar of three half stitches to reach to 4. Pass the right-hand leadwork pair through the nearest two pairs from the block made with the pairs from C and D. Leave the leadwork pair and work three half stitches with the other two pairs to reach to 4, where another block is made as above.

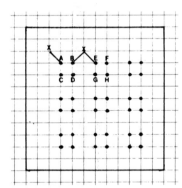

Filling 3: Jubilee

FILLING 3: JUBILEE

(See Sampler diagram.) Sew two pairs above A and two pairs above B. Work a whole stitch and three twists with the two left-hand pairs and set pin A between them. Work a whole stitch and three twists with the two right-hand pairs and set pin B between them. With the two middle pairs work a whole stitch and three twists (No Pin). With the two left-hand pairs work a whole stitch and three twists and set pin C between them. With the two right-hand pairs work a whole stitch and three twists and set pin D between them. With the two middle pairs work a whole stitch and three twists (No Pin). Enclose pins C and D with a whole stitch and three twists. Work the next group of four holes E, F, G and H as above. Work the two pairs from D through the two pairs from G in whole stitch. Twist all four pairs three times.

Each two pairs are now in position to work the next groups of four holes diagonally below, together with the two new pairs coming in from each side.

FILLING 4: NO PIN

(See Sampler diagram.) No pricking is needed for this filling, as the name suggests. It consists of rows of small square leadworks.

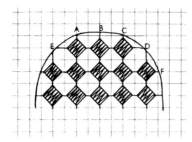

Filling 4: No Pin

Sew one pair into each hole (or if the holes are very close together, into every other hole) in a straight line across the top of the space to be filled, and one pair on the right-hand side (at D on the diagram, usually the next hole slightly below C). Twist all pairs three times. Use the left-hand bobbin from D as the weaver for the first leadwork and take it under, over and back under the next two bobbins (from C). * It is now in the right position to weave the leadwork. When this has been completed, the weaver is again the second bobbin from the left. Twist both pairs three times. This brings the weaver to lie as the outer bobbin on the left. Leave the right-hand pair and work the next leadwork with the left-hand pair and the pair from B, *again using the same weaver*, which is first passed under, over and back under the two bobbins from B. Repeat from * across the row and after working the last leadwork, sew out the left-hand pair (containing the runner, see note **20d**) at E. If the shape being filled curves, as in the diagram, sew in a new pair at D and one at F. Twist both pairs three times and work another row of leadworks. The pair sewn out at E may also be brought in again and twisted three times to make an extra leadwork if needed.

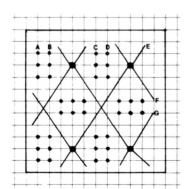

Filling 5: Snatch Bar with Leadworks

FILLING 5: SNATCH BAR WITH LEADWORKS

(See Sampler diagram.) Sew in two pairs above A and three pairs above B, C and D. If the six holes of the snatch bar are a little way away from the edge at which the pairs have been sewn in, work a whole stitch and one twist with the two pairs from A and the next two pairs from B, and use these four pairs to work the snatch bar as follows. Take the right-hand pair of the four as runners through the other three pairs in whole stitch, twist the runners seven times and set pin A under them. Take the runners back through three pairs, twist them seven times and set pin B under them. Continue working the runners back and forth, twisting round the pins, until all six holes have been used. After the last hole work the runners back through three pairs, then twist the runners and the last pair they passed through once. Work a whole stitch and one twist with the other two pairs and leave. Work the next vertical snatch bar, using the two right-hand pairs from C and two left-hand pairs from D. Twist the two pairs remaining above B and C six times and use them to make a square leadwork. Twist the pairs six times again after the leadwork is completed and leave. The weaver in every leadwork must finish in the left-hand pair of the leadwork.

After completing the leadworks, lengthen the pairs that have made them so that they may be recognised subsequently. Work a similar leadwork with the pairs from above D and E. The right-hand pair of the leadwork is sewn out at F and brought in again. (This pair need not be lengthened.)

Sew in another new pair at F and three pairs at G. Four pairs now make a horizontal snatch bar in the same way as the vertical ones. The pairs of this snatch bar are now worked through the pairs of the snatch bar from CD with the leadwork pairs between as follows. Take the left-hand pair of the FG snatch bar in whole stitch through the left-hand pair of the DE leadwork (this contains the weaver, so work carefully) and through the four pairs of the CD snatch bar, and leave. Take the right-hand pair of the CD snatch bar through the DE leadwork pair and through the three remaining pairs of the FG snatch, and leave. * Take the first pair lying on the right of the DE leadwork pair through the leadwork pair and through two more pairs to the left and leave. Take the first pair lying on the left of the DE leadwork pair through the leadwork pair and through two more pairs to the right and leave. * Take the right-hand pair from the BC leadwork in whole stitch through all nine pairs to the right and leave it to work the leadwork in the square below later. Take the first pair lying on the right of the DE leadwork pair in whole stitch through the leadwork pair and through two pairs to the left and leave. Take the first pair lying on the left of the DE leadwork pair in whole stitch through the leadwork pair and through one pair to the right. Take the first pair lying on the right of the DE leadwork in whole stitch through the leadwork pair and one pair to the left and leave. Take the first pair lying on the left of the DE leadwork in whole stitch through the leadwork pair and leave. This completes the crossing.

The four pairs of the CD snatch are now in position to work the next snatch bar below them, but before this can be worked, make a whole stitch and one twist with each two pairs. Similarly, the pairs of the FG snatch bar will work the next horizontal snatch bar and the leadwork pair left in position to work the leadwork below this later, together with another pair coming from the left.

FILLING 6: FOUR PIN
(See Sampler diagram.) Sew in two pairs above each hole A, B, E, F, G and H. The four pairs from above A and B work the first group of four holes as follows. * With the two left-hand pairs work a whole stitch, twist both pairs three times, and set pin A between them. With the two right-hand pairs work a whole stitch,

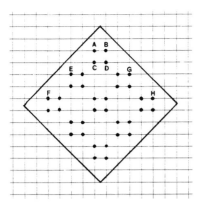

Filling 6: Four Pin

twist both pairs three times and set pin B between them. With the two middle pairs work a whole stitch and twist both pairs three times (No Pin). With the two left-hand pairs work a whole stitch, twist both pairs three times and set pin C between them. With the two right-hand pairs work a whole stitch, twist both pairs three times and set pin D between them. With the two middle pairs work a whole stitch and twist both pairs three times (No Pin). * The two left-hand pairs and the two pairs from above E now work the next group of four holes * to *, and at the end the two left-hand pairs from this group meet the two pairs from above F to work the next group of four holes. Continue down this diagonal line until the row is complete; at the end, sew out the left-hand two pairs. Return to the top and work the next group of holes with the two pairs from above G and the two pairs from D. Continue down this diagonal line, using the two left-hand pairs of each group with the pairs left from the previous line of four pins.

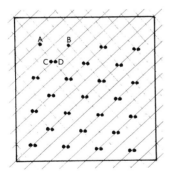

Filling 7: Whole Stitch Block Variation

FILLING 7: WHOLE STITCH BLOCK VARIATION

(See Sampler diagram.) Four pairs are required to work each group of two holes. Sew in two pairs at A and B. Work a half stitch plait with each two pairs to reach to just above C and D. * Use the second pair from the right of these four pairs as runners and take them in whole stitch through two pairs to the left. Twist the runners seven times and set pin C under them. Work the runners through three pairs to the right, twist them seven times and set pin D under them. Work the runners through two pairs to the left and leave. With each two pairs work a half stitch plait to the group diagonally below (four half stitches should be enough), where they repeat the procedure from *, together with two pairs coming from the other side.

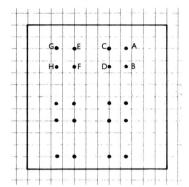

Filling 8: Blossom

FILLING 8: BLOSSOM

(See Sampler diagram.) The pricking is the same as for Jubilee filling, but as this filling is worked from right to left, the lettering is different. Refer to the Blossom diagram. Sew two pairs into the edge of the braid half-way between and above C and A. Sew in two pairs half-way between and to the right of A and B. Work a half stitch plait with each set of two pairs just to reach as far as the group of four holes. The four holes of each group are used to make purls as follows.

Use the right-hand pair of the left-hand plait to make a purl in hole A, * twisting this pair seven times, using the right-hand bobbin to make the loop, and placing the pin under the right-hand thread, pointing to the left, twisting the point over the thread towards you and down into the hole. Lift the other thread round the pin from right to left. Twist the pair once. * Make a whole stitch with the two left-hand pairs and twist both pairs once. With the two centre pairs make a whole stitch and twist both pairs once. With the two right-hand pairs make a whole stitch and use the right of these two pairs to make a purl in hole B * to *.

Make a whole stitch with the two right-hand pairs. With the two left-hand pairs make a whole stitch and use the left of these pairs to make a purl in hole C, ** twisting this pair seven times. Place the pin under the left-hand bobbin, pointing towards the right. Twist the point over the thread towards you and down into the hole. Lift the other thread round the pin from left to right. Twist the pair twice (left over right). ** Work a whole stitch with the two left-hand pairs. Twist the two centre pairs once and make a whole stitch with them. Work a whole stitch with the two right-hand pairs. Use the left of these two pairs to make a purl at D, repeating ** to **. This completes one group of holes.

The two pairs between C and D now make a half stitch plait to reach as far as E, where they work the next group of four holes together with the two pairs sewn in above G and E. Put aside the two pairs between D and B. Continue along this row from right to left and after the last group of holes work a half stitch plait to reach the edge, where these two pairs are sewn out. With the two pairs put aside and left hanging below each group of holes, work half stitch plaits to reach the group of holes below. Sew two more pairs in on the right-hand side, and work a half stitch plait to the next set of holes.

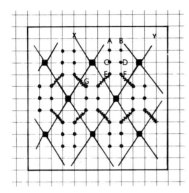

Filling 9: Toad in the Hole

FILLING 9: TOAD IN THE HOLE

(See Sampler diagram.) Sew in one pair above X and Y and three pairs each above A and B. The pair from X and the left-hand pair from A are each twisted five times and used to make a square leadwork after which they are twisted five times again and left. The right-hand pair from B and the pair from Y are left to work a similar leadwork in the next row. With the two pairs from above A work a whole stitch and one twist. Do the same with the two pairs from above B.

To work the group of six holes, or 'snatch' (as it is called in Devon) use the right-hand pair of these four as runners, and work them through three pairs to the left in whole stitch. Twist the runners seven times, set pin A under them and continue working the runners back and forth to B, C, D, E and F, twisting seven times round each pin. After F has been set, work back through three pairs, twist the runners and the last pair they passed through once and leave them. Work a whole stitch and one twist with the other two pairs and leave. This completes the snatch.

The right-hand pair of the leadwork now works through the two left-hand pairs of the snatch in whole stitch, and is now left for a leadwork in the next row. With the two pairs from the snatch through which the leadwork pair has passed, work a whole stitch and one twist. The right-hand pair of these two becomes the runner pair for the next snatch. This is worked with these two pairs and two more coming in from the other side, either from another snatch or sewn in at the side of the space. The snatch is begun by working the runners through three pairs to the left, twisting them seven times and setting pin G under them. The other two pairs from the first snatch are left to work a snatch in the next row, after a leadwork pair has passed through them. It is best to work this filling in diagonal rows from top right to bottom left.

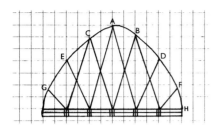

Filling 10: Italian

FILLING 10: ITALIAN

(See Sampler diagram.) This is worked without a pricking. Sew in pairs as indicated in the diagram. The pairs across the top are sewn in at every hole, or if the holes are very close together at every other hole. Make a whole stitch and three twists with each two pairs from A, B and C. With the right-hand pair from A and the left-hand pair from B work a whole stitch and three twists. With the left-hand pair from A and the right-hand pair from C work a whole stitch and three twists. Twist the pair from D three times and use it with the right-hand pair from B to work a whole stitch and three twists. Twist the pair from E three times and use it with the left-hand pair from C to work a whole stitch and three twists. Twist the pair from F three times and use it with the next pair on the left to work a whole stitch. Do not twist. Work a whole stitch with the next two pairs on the left; leave these, work another whole stitch with the next two pairs on the left, and so on across the row. The odd pair at the end is joined by the pair from G which has first been twisted three times.

There are now complete sets of four bobbins across the row and complete diamonds have been formed above these. The pair sewn in at H now becomes the runner pair for the horizontal rows dividing the diamonds. Twist this pair three times, * work it in whole stitch through the next set of two pairs, twist the runners three times again and repeat from * across the row, sewing the runner pair into the braid at the other side, after pulling it up well. Ensure the line is horizontal and the pairs through which the runners pass are not twisted.

After sewing, tie the runners once, twist them three times and work a return row as above, again sewing the runners in at the right-hand side into hole H. Occasionally, if the first line is not quite straight, the second sewing may be made into the next hole below H. Again, twist the runners three times and work another row as the first, sewing them out at the end and into the same hole as the first sewing on that side. This completes one repeat of the pattern. The runners may be needed for the twisted diamond work, otherwise they are tied three times and laid back to be cut off later.

The next set of diamonds is worked as above and is started by working a whole stitch and three twists with each set of four bobbins hanging below the last horizontal bar. The diamond work at the sides will vary according to the shape of the space; the odd pairs at the sides will either be sewn in at the sides, twisted three times, and brought back again to work with any odd pairs, or an extra pair may need to be sewn in, to use with the odd pair at the sides to form extra diamonds in a widening space. There must be complete sets of four bobbins ready before the horizontal line is worked.

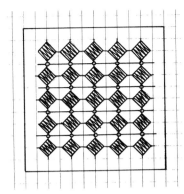

Filling 11: Swing and a Pin

FILLING 11: SWING AND A PIN

(See Sampler diagram.) The holes needed for this filling are pricked in as the filling progresses. The first row consists of leadworks, which are sewn in and made in exactly the same way as described for No Pin (filling 4).

The rows of leadworks alternate with rows in which a twisted pair is worked through the leadwork pairs and pin holes are made, as follows. Sew in one pair at the right-hand edge immediately below the level of the leadworks. Twist this pair three times and work a whole stitch with the pair from the nearest leadwork. Twist both pairs three times. * Prick a hole immediately below the leadwork and set a pin into it between these two pairs. Enclose the pin with a whole stitch and three twists. Leave the right-hand pair and with the left-hand pair and the next pair on the left work a whole stitch and three twists. Repeat from * across the row. Ensure that the pin holes are pricked in a straight line. Sew out the left-hand pairs at the left side. The next row is a leadwork row.

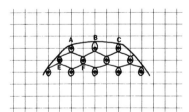

Filling 12: Pin and a Stitch

FILLING 12: PIN AND A STITCH

(See Sampler diagram.) Sew in two pairs above each hole along the top line. With each two pairs work a whole stitch and three twists and set pins between them, enclosing the pins with a whole stitch and three twists. The pairs now divide to work the holes diagonally below them, the right-hand pair from A and the left-hand pair from B working hole F, etc., as above. The left-hand pair from A meets a new pair sewn in at the edge and twisted three times, to work hole E.

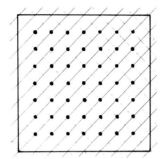

Filling 13: Pin and a Chain

FILLING 13: PIN AND A CHAIN

(See Sampler diagram.) This consists of a pin hole row and a row made with a twisted pair alternating. Sew in two pairs above each hole along the top. With each two pairs work a whole stitch, twist both pairs three times, set a pin between them and enclose the pin with a whole stitch. Do not twist. This completes the first horizontal row of holes.

Sew in a new pair at the right-hand side, between the row of holes just worked and the next row. Twist this pair three times, and use it as a runner pair to work in whole stitch through the two pairs which enclosed the nearest pin. * Twist the runners three times and work them through the next two pairs in whole stitch, repeat from * across the row and sew out the runners at the end after twisting them three times and pulling up well. The next row is a pinhole row and is worked like the first.

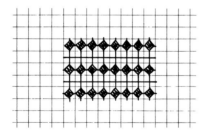

Filling 14: Swing and a Stitch

FILLING 14: SWING AND A STITCH

(See Sampler diagram.) This filling needs no pricking and is similar to Swing and a Pin (filling **11**). It consists of rows of leadworks and rows made with a twisted pair alternating. Work the first row of leadworks as explained in No Pin (filling **4**). Sew in a new pair at the right-hand edge immediately below the level of the leadworks. Twist this pair three times and work a whole stitch with the nearest leadwork pair, * twist both pairs three times, leave the right-hand pair and with the left-hand pair and the next leadwork pair work a whole stitch. Repeat from * across the row and sew out the left-hand pair at the end of the row, after pulling it as much as possible into a straight line below the leadworks.

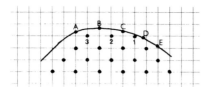

Filling 15: Trolly Net

FILLING 15: TROLLY NET

(See Sampler diagram.) This filling is worked in horizontal rows. (Prick diagonally for a smaller mesh.) Sew in one pair at A, B and C above and between each two holes of the filling. Sew in one pair at D on the right-hand side level with the first row of holes. Twist all pairs two or three times according to the distance between the pin holes and the edge of the braid. With the pairs from D and C work a half stitch, twist both pairs four times and set pin 1 between them. * Leave the right-hand pair, and with the left-hand pair and the pair from B work another half stitch and four twists. Set a pin between these pairs. Repeat from * across the row, using the next pair on the left for each stitch. Sew out the left-hand pair at the end of the row. Sew in a new pair at E, twist it and use it with the pair from 1 to work a half stitch and four twists. Set a pin between these pairs. Repeat from * above. The threads run in a diagonal line from top left to bottom right.

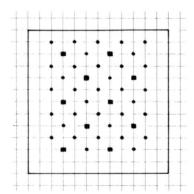

Filling 16: Spotted Net

FILLING 16: SPOTTED NET

(See pattern **41**: Roses and Lilies Floral Mat.) Work the first row as above. In the next row leadworks alternate with net stitches. The leadworks take the place of one pin hole and are made with the pairs which would normally have made this pin hole. The position of the leadworks may be marked on the pricking before beginning work. The weaver for the leadwork is the second bobbin from the right of the four threads, and it is passed under the next thread on the left, and over and back under the next thread, to bring it into the correct position to begin weaving. After the leadwork is finished, twist both pairs three times, so that the weaver becomes the last thread on the left of the four, and remains the leading thread and weaver for the whole row. The next row is a net row, and in the following row the leadworks come in alternate spaces to the last leadwork row.

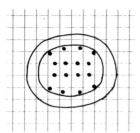

Filling 17: Cartwheel

FILLING 17: CARTWHEEL

(See pattern **25**: Large Flower Spray.) This is often used as a filling for a flower or for a round or oval space. It can be made with six, eight or ten leadworks. Sew two pairs for each leadwork into two adjacent braid holes above the single holes at the top of the filling. With each two pairs make a whole stitch, twist both pairs three times and set pins between them. With each two pairs work a narrow leadwork to the middle row of holes. Twist all pairs three times and set pins between each two pairs into the top row of the holes in the middle. * Leave the outside pair on each side and join all other adjoining pairs with a whole stitch and three twists. * Laying each pair with its original partner (i.e. bringing in the two outer pairs), work a whole stitch and three twists with each two pairs, and set pins between each two pairs into the lower row of holes in the middle. Repeat from * to *. Work a leadwork with each two pairs to the holes at the lower edge, twist each pair three times, set pins between them and work a whole stitch. Make three twists if the holes are a little distance from the braid, and sew out.

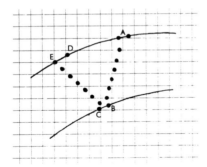

Filling 18: Purl Pin Bars

FILLING 18: PURL PIN BARS

(See pattern **3**: Shell.) These are made with four pairs which are sewn into two adjacent holes at A. With the first pair on the right, work through the other three pairs to the left, twist the runners once and leave them. * Use the last pair the runners worked through as new runners to work through two pairs to the right. Use this pair to make a purl on the right side of the bar, twisting it seven times, placing a pin under the outer thread, pointing towards the left, and twisting the pin over the thread towards you and down into the first pin hole. Twist the second thread up round the pin from right to left and pull up. Twist the pair once and work back with this pair through three pairs to the left, twist the runners once and leave them. Repeat from *.

When the bar has reached the opposite braid and the last purl has been made, work the runners back to the left and through to the purl edge again and sew them to the braid at B. Work one whole stitch with the sewn pair and the next pair on the left, leave the left of these two pairs, and sew the right-hand pair at C. Tie this pair once, and use it as the runner to work the next bar. When the last purl of the second bar has been made, work the runners to the plain side and sew them at D. Work a whole stitch with the sewn pair and the next pair on the right, leave the right of these pairs and sew the left pair at E. The purls are usually made on the right side of each bar, but they may be worked on the left. or the left and right on alternate bars.

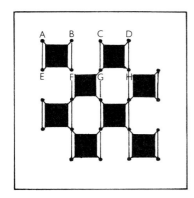

Filling 19: Brick

FILLING 19: BRICK

(See pattern **23**: Plain Mat with Fillings.) Sew two pairs above each hole across the top of the pattern. With each two pairs make a whole stitch and twist both pairs three times. Set a pin between each two pairs in the holes below them, and enclose the pin with a whole stitch and three twists. With the right-hand pair from A and the left-hand pair from B make a leadwork. Repeat with the right-hand pair from C and the left-hand pair from D. Twist all the leadwork pairs three times. With the pair hanging from A and the nearest leadwork pair * make a whole stitch, twist both pairs three times, set pin E between them and enclose the pin with a whole stitch and three twists *. Repeat from * to * across the row with each two pairs (pins F, G, H, etc.). In the next row leadworks are made in alternate spaces (e.g. the right-hand pair from F and the left-hand pair from G make a leadwork) and at the end, the leadwork pairs are joined to the pairs hanging on either side, and the next row of pins is set as above.

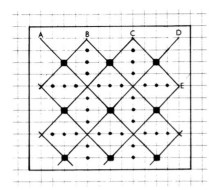

Filling 20: Rib Squares and Leadwork

FILLING 20: RIB SQUARES AND LEADWORK

(See pattern **40**: Mat with Spotted Net.) Sew in a pair at A and at D. Sew in six pairs (three into each of two adjacent holes) at B and six pairs at C. Sew in four pairs (two into each of two adjacent holes) at E. With the right outer pair from C and the pair from D, each twisted five times, work a square leadwork. Twist the pairs five times again and leave. Work similar leadwork with the left outer pair from C and the right outer pair from B. With the four pairs left at C work a rib (note **18**) with the pin holes on the right, down the three holes below C. Leave. Work the right-hand pair from CD leadwork in whole stitch through the four pairs from E and leave it to work a leadwork in the space below later. With the four pairs from E work the three horizontal holes in rib with the pin holes on the right.

The pairs from the vertical and horizontal ribs are now crossed, together with two leadwork pairs as follows. Lengthen the two threads of the left-hand pair of the CD leadwork (this contains the weaver so be careful not to draw up the leadwork) and lay this pair over the four pairs of the vertical rib from C. Now lift the four pairs of the horizontal rib completely over the other five pairs. The four pairs of the rib from E are now on the left, then comes the leadwork pair and the four pairs of the rib from C are on the right. Now take the right-hand pair from the BC leadwork in whole stitch through the nine crossed pairs, pull up this pair and the crossed pairs well and leave. Leave the leadwork pair on the right to use later for the leadwork, together with the pair from E. This completes one repeat of the pattern.

Begin the next repeat by working the leadwork with the pair from A and the outer left-hand pair from B. Then the three vertical holes of rib from B and the three horizontal holes of the rib with the four left-hand pairs of those from the last crossing. In these instructions the ribs have been worked with the pin holes on the right of each rib, but they may equally well be made on the left. They should always be made on the same side throughout a filling.

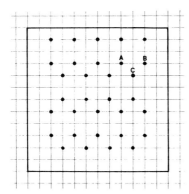

Filling 21: Straight Pin

FILLING 21: STRAIGHT PIN

(See pattern **19**: Butterfly with Trolly Net.) Sew two pairs above each hole across the top of the pattern; with each two pairs make a whole stitch, twist both pairs three times and set pins into the holes between them. With each two pairs work a narrow leadwork to reach the pin holes in the next row. Twist the pairs three times and set a pin between the pairs of each leadwork. Enclose the pins with a whole stitch and twist both pairs three times. The right-hand pair from A and the left-hand pair from B now meet and repeat the pattern (i.e. make a whole stitch and three twists, set pin C between them and use them to make another leadwork). The remaining pairs from A and B meet a pair coming from each side.

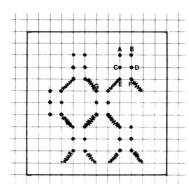

Filling 22: Whole Stitch Block

FILLING 22: WHOLE STITCH BLOCK

(See pattern **17**: Culm Edging, and filling **9**: Toad in the Hole.) The blocks or 'snatches' are worked as in Toad in the Hole (filling **9**). Four pairs are sewn in above each snatch hole and a whole stitch and one twist is made with each two pairs before beginning to work the snatch. After the last pin of the snatch has been set, work the runners through to the outer side once more, twist them and the last pair they passed through once and leave them. The other two pairs make a whole stitch and twist once. The right-hand pair of the two from E becomes the runner pair for the next snatch diagonally below and works through three pairs to the left before twisting round pin G.

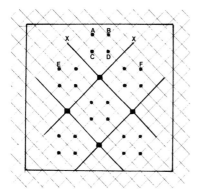

Filling 23: Four Pin and Leadwork

FILLING 23: FOUR PIN AND LEADWORK

(See pattern **17**: Culm Edging.) Sew in two pairs above each hole A, B, E and F and one pair at each point X. Using the four pairs above A and B, work the first group of four holes as follows. * With the two left-hand pairs work a whole stitch, twist both pairs three times and set pin A between them. With the two right-hand pairs work a whole stitch, twist both pairs three times and set pin B between them. With the two middle pairs work a whole stitch and twist both pairs three times (No Pin). With the two left-hand pairs work a whole stitch, twist both pairs three times and set pin C between them. With the two right-hand pairs work a whole stitch, twist both pairs three times and set pin D between them. With the two middle pairs work a whole stitch and twist both pairs three times (No Pin). * Now enclose pins C and D with a whole stitch. Twist the pairs from X three times and work them in whole stitch through the pairs from C and D, so that they meet in the space below the first group of holes, where they are twisted three times and work a square leadwork. Twist both pairs three times after the leadwork and leave them. The pairs from C and E work the next four pin group from * to *, after which the two lower pairs are enclosed with a whole stitch, and the left-hand pair of the leadwork is worked in whole stitch through the two right-hand pairs of this group.

FILLING 24: TOAD IN THE HOLE WITH WIDE LEADWORK

(See pattern **16**: Brunswick Edging.) This is similar to Toad in the Hole (filling **9**), but the leadwork pairs are omitted, the leadwork being made with the runners from adjacent snatches half way through the snatch. Work horizontally as follows. Four pairs are sewn in above each whole stitch block or snatch, and a whole stitch and twist is made with each two pairs before beginning the snatch. The runners are the right-hand pair of each set of four and they work back and forth through the other three, as shown in the diagram, seven twists

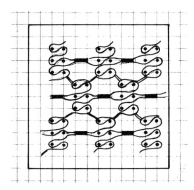

Filling 24: Toad in the Hole with Wide Leadwork

being made round each pin, except the middle pins. When the middle pin in each of two adjacent snatches has been set, the runner pairs are twisted three times and meet to make a wide, shallow leadwork, after which they are twisted three times again, and each continues to weave its own snatch.

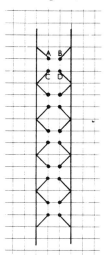

Filling 25: Four Pin with Half Stitch Bars

FILLING 25: FOUR PIN WITH HALF STITCH BARS

(See pattern 10: Cross, and pattern 18: Bow.) This is used to fill a long, narrow space, being composed of groups of four pins, the pairs being attached to the edges of the braid between groups of holes. Sew two pairs into the braid on each side, diagonally above the group of four holes, then work a half stitch plait with each set of two to form a bar to reach the group of holes. * The last stitch of the bar should be a whole stitch, each pair being twisted three times before pins A and B are set between them. With the two middle pairs, work a whole stitch and three twists (No Pin). With the two left-hand pairs, work a whole stitch and three twists, and set pin C between them. With the two right-hand pairs, work a whole stitch and three twists, and set pin D between them. With the two middle pairs, work a whole stitch and three twists (No Pin). Each two pairs now work a half stitch bar to reach to the edges of the braid half way between the sets of holes, where they are sewn, tied once (to hold the bar firm), and then used to work a bar to the next set of holes. Repeat from *.

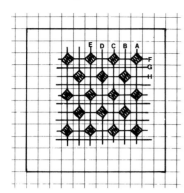

Filling 26: Devonshire Cutwork

FILLING 26: DEVONSHIRE CUTWORK (SWING AND A STITCH VARIATION)

(See pattern **15**: Exe Edging.) No pricking is needed. Sew in one pair at every hole or, if the holes are close together, at every other hole, across the top of the space, and one pair on the right side at F, one hole below A. Twist all pairs three times. The left-hand bobbin of the pair from F is the weaver for the leadwork. * It is taken under the next thread on the left and over and back under the next thread, to bring it into the right position to begin weaving a small square leadwork. When this is finished and both pairs have been twisted three times, the weaver is the outer thread on the left of these four. Leave the right-hand pair and with the left-hand pair and the pair from B work a whole stitch and three twists. Pull up the stitch carefully. Leave the right-hand pair and with the left-hand pair and the pair from C make another leadwork, using the same weaver as for the previous leadwork. This is the second thread from the right of these four. Repeat from * across the row, sewing in the pair which has woven across at the end. For the next row a new pair is sewn in at G, and this is twisted three times. Work a whole stitch and three twists (both pairs) with each pair across the row, after which it is pulled up carefully into a straight line and sewn out on the other side. In the following row the leadworks are made with the pair which made a stitch in the first row, so that they come in alternate spaces and a new pair is sewn in at H to work this row.

8 ⚏ Leaves

LEAF 1: DIVIDED LEAF

(See Sampler diagram.) Begin at the bottom of the leaf and work the braid in the usual way, using the edge holes on the outside and the vein holes on the inside, and reduce the number of pairs as the work narrows near the top of the leaf. It will be necessary to back stitch in the last two or three holes on the vein side and the top vein hole should always be a back stitch which is not made up (i.e. the edge stitch not worked) until the top of the leaf has been turned. From here the runners work to the top outer hole of the leaf and make the edge stitch. Take the runners back through the coarse pair and tie them once before going on. Turn the pillow.

The procedure now varies according to whether any outside holes have to be worked to bring the work level with the top vein hole. If no outer holes need to be worked, take the tied runners through all the downrights and make up the back stitch in the top vein hole. If one outer hole has to be worked, take the tied runners through all downrights except the coarse pair, * leave the runners and use the last pair worked through as new runners to work to the outer edge and make the edge stitch. On return, work through all downrights and make up the back stitch in the top vein hole. * If two outer holes have to be worked, take the tied runners to within one pair of the coarse pair, leave the runners and use the last pair they worked through as new runners to work to the outer edge and make up the edge stitch. On return, work through all downrights except the coarse pair and repeat from * to *.

Having made up the back stitch in the top vein hole, take the runners back to the outer edge, make the edge stitch and leave. Untwist the edge pair on the inner side and slip the coarse thread through (over and under) this pair – no edge pair will now be needed on this side. The coarse thread will hang next to the sewing. The second half of the leaf is usually worked in half stitch from here. Take the runners from the outside edge through all downrights (no twist at the end of the row) and sew them into the vein hole below the top one. Replace the pin after sewing, work to the outer edge with the sewn runners, make the edge stitch and leave.

Remove the pin from the top vein hole and pull the inner coarse thread *gently*. This has the effect of flattening the work round the top vein hole where the threads tend to bunch. Continue the braid, making edge holes on the outer side and sewing into the vein holes on the inner side. In lieu of back stitches on the inner side, sew twice into the same hole where necessary.

LEAF 2: CENTRE LEADWORK AND PIN

(See Sampler diagram.) Set up at the top of the leaf with six pairs and a coarse pair and work three rows in whole stitch, then add one pair at each hole (fourteen pairs), then divide. Leave the runners at the outside edge and divide the pairs so that there are seven on each side. Take the four centre bobbins (one pair from each side) and make a whole stitch with them. Work the runners from the edge through to the middle and through the nearest of the two centre pairs. Twist the runners seven times and set a pin under them into the top hole of the division. Work back with these runners to the same edge and work an edge stitch there. Work back to the middle again, twist the runners seven times, set a pin under them in the next hole and leave them.

Take the remaining centre pair and use as runners to work to the other side, where the usual edge is made, then work back to the middle, twist seven times and set a pin under them. Each runner pair now works back to the edge on its own side and returns to the middle again; twist the runners three times, set a pin under each and use them to make a leadwork. Again, twist these pairs three times and work each runner pair out to its edge again. Continue the leaf, alternating pin holes and leadworks in the middle. The vein may be closed like the ladder trail (leaf **7**), but in the sampler two halves are sewn out separately.

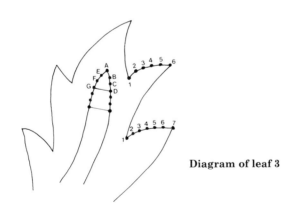

Diagram of leaf 3

LEAF 3: RIB, LEADWORK CENTRE AND POINTS

(See Sampler diagram, and diagram for leaf **3**.) Start the rib which forms each side of the central vein by hanging ten pairs round a pin in hole A. Twist all pairs twice. Work a whole stitch with the two outer pairs on the left side and twist both pairs three times. The inner pair of these works through all but the last pair on the right side. Set pin B under the runners and work the normal edge stitch with the last pair. Now divide the bobbins into two halves with five pairs in each half. Take the innermost pair from each half and work a whole stitch with these. Work the runners through to the middle including the nearest pair from the central whole stitch. Twist the runners once and leave them. Work back with the last pair the runners passed through and make the next hole of the rib at C. Work one more row of rib, working to hole D.

The rib on the other side is begun by taking the remaining pair of the centre whole stitch as runners to E and making an edge stitch there. Work two more rows of rib on this side using holes F and G. From D and G bring the runner pair of each side through to the middle and use these to make a shallow leadwork (twist each pair once before and after the leadwork). Work each runner back to its own pin hole side and continue ribs making a leadwork after each third pin. Sew out the ribs at the end.

Set up again at the outer tip of the leaf with six pairs; a coarse pair may be used although none was used in the sampler. Work down to the point of centre rib in whole stitch, adding pairs on both sides. When the work is level with the top of the vein the pairs are divided. Work the runners to the middle and sew them (note **20f**) into hole A. Sew the next pair of downrights into the same hole, tie it once and use it as the runner pair for the other side. Each side is now worked independently, making edge holes on the outer sides and taking top sewings on the vein side. Work the right side first. The rows of weaving must be kept level so that when the hole at the base of the first point is reached, the sewings in the vein side have not dropped below this level (in this case hole B, which will be used twice, once before the point is started and again when it is finished).

When pin 1 has been set, hang in two new pairs, laying these inside the coarse thread, and make up the edge stitch. Work through the coarse pair and one more pair, leave the runners and use the last pair they passed through to work to hole 2. Before making up the edge stitch here, hang in two new pairs which are laid inside the coarse thread and one pair which is laid to the back of the pillow. (Count the first downright pair as coarse pair.)

* Make up the edge stitch, work back through the coarse pair, tie the runners once and work them through one more pair. Leave the runners and use the last pair they worked through as new runners to work to 3. Two more pairs are added here and laid inside the coarse thread. Repeat from * for holes 4 and 5. After making the edge stitch at 5 work through the coarse pair and tie the runners once, then take the tied runners through seven pairs to hole 2. Leave the runners and tie the last pair they passed through once. Use this pair as new runners to work to 6. Make the edge here. Bring the pair which was laid to the back of the pillow to the front and lay it to the left of the old runner pair left at 2. This fills in the tiny gap caused by the turn here in the last row. Tie the runners after they have passed through the coarse pair and then take them through all pairs to the centre vein, where they are sewn to hole B. Continue working the leaf taking out a pair at the next and several subsequent holes as the point narrows.

The method of working the point varies from the above description according to the shape of the point. For instance, the next point on this side is much sharper than the first. In this case, two pairs were hung in at 1 and 2, three pairs were hung in at 3, one of these being laid to the back of the pillow, and three more at 4, again putting one of these back. One pair was added at 5 and one at 6. From the point of 7 work back through five pairs to hole 4, tie the last pair passed through, leave the runners and use the tied pair to work to the outer edge. Here the pair next to the coarse thread is taken out, and before working back to hole 3 bring in the pair lack back at 4. Work out to the edge again, take a pair out, bring in the pair laid back at 3 and then work back through all pairs to the rib in the middle. The other point is worked similarly and the section is sewn out into the scroll. The other side is begun with the pair sewn in at A and worked in the same way. Half stitch may also be used for this leaf.

LEAF 4: SIMPLE RAISED LEAF

(See Sampler diagram.) Sew seven pairs into the stem at the base of the leaf and work a rib up the outer edge of the leaf. After setting the third pin from the tip of the leaf, and before making up the edge stitch, add a new pair. Bring this pair up around the pin as usual but do not lay it into the rib; lay it to the back of the pillow. Make the edge stitch, add another new pair at the next pin, laying it beside the first. After making the edge stitch and before working the next row of rib, take the first downright pair past the pin and lay it beside the other two pairs at the back (keep these pairs in the order in which they were laid aside). Work the last row of rib and set the pin in the top hole of the leaf. Turn the pillow after working the edge stitch.

Work the runners through the first downright pair and tie them once to keep this pair well up against the pin at the point. Continue with the tied runners through all the downright pairs, through the pair which was laid back and through the second of the new pairs which were added. Before taking the runners through this pair, tie it once to prevent it from slipping. This should be done with all laid in pairs before they are worked. Leave the runners and tie the last pair they passed through once. Use this tied pair as new runners to work to the outer edge and make the edge stitch. Work to the rib side again through all pairs, including the first new pair which was laid in. Leave the runners and tie the last pair through which they passed once. Use this tied pair as new runners to work towards the outer edge through three pairs. Twist the runner once to open the vein in the centre of the row and continue to the edge, where a new pair is added.

From now on top sewings must be made whenever the runners reach the rib side, the first of these being made in the fourth hole from the top. The runners are twisted twice and then three times in the next two rows to increase the width of the vein in the centre, and these three twists are continued; twist twice and then once to close the vein at the end of the leaf.

Three pairs are taken out after the vein is closed. After the last hole has been used and the runners taken across and sewn into the rib, sew the edge pair on the plain side into the rib of the stem and tie it three times. Tie the sewn runners on the rib side three times. These seven pairs are now in position to work the rib up the side of the second leaf. When this is completed it is sewn out into its own rib and into the rib of the main stem.

When trying to decide where and when to begin adding new pairs to lay aside for filling in later, imagine that you are starting the leaf in the normal way from the tip and adding new pairs as the leaf widens. On one side, these are the positions where new pairs are laid in on the rib. Any new pairs needed on the other side will be added when working down the leaf later. This applies not only to leaves but to any raised, shaped section, such as petals, etc.

LEAF 5: LEAF WITH RAISED VEINS

(See Sampler diagram, and diagram for leaf **5**.) The raised vein is worked first and the half stitch leaf is worked afterwards in two parts. Begin at the top of the vein with seven pairs at A and work a rib with the pin holes on the right-hand side, finishing at pin B, where two pairs are hung in and placed inside the first downright thread, before the edge stitch is made. To work the first side

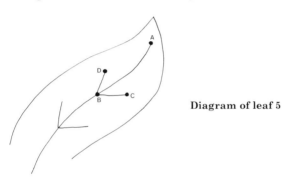

Diagram of leaf 5

vein lay the edge pairs of the rib aside *under* the four left-hand pairs and use these four pairs to work a rib to top hole C, with the pin holes on the left (i.e. facing the base of the leaf). After the edge stitch at C, take leaders through to the plain side of the rib, tie them twice, lay all three pairs of the rib between them and tie them twice again over the pairs.

These pairs are now rolled down to B on the pin hole side. One pair can be left behind to attach the roll (note **20g**), or the roll can be sewn as it is being made, with the rolling pair, to each pin hole in turn. Do not sew at B. Lift the four pairs of the branch just made and lay them between the two bobbins of the nearest downright pair on the left (not the edge pair which was laid aside, after edge stitch B was made). Tie this downright pair twice over the four pairs of the side vein. Make another rib to D, using the four left-hand pairs and making pin holes on the right. Tie and roll back as before, lay these pairs between the bobbins of the nearest downright pair and tie it over them twice. Tie three times any two pairs except the edge pair of the rib and cut off; continue the main rib to where the next side veins are to be made.

If the side veins do not come exactly opposite each other, they are worked as described above, but there is no need to hang in any extra pairs. The rib is sewn out at the base. Set up again at the top of the leaf, add a coarse pair here and work in half stitch to where the vein starts. Divide the downright pairs allowing more pairs to work the wider side. Work the runners to A and sew the runner – the leading thread of the last half stitch – to A (note **20f**) and when the loop has been drawn through, put the *same* bobbins, i.e. the runner through the loop, tightening the loop carefully and easing it down with the needlepin, so that it does not lock on the thread until it has reached the pin hole. This type of sewing also applies when the backing is made in whole stitch. Sew the next downright pair into the same hole and use it as a runner for the other side of the leaf. Both sides are now worked independently, making pin holes on the outer side and top sewings on the vein side. When the tops of the side veins are reached the runner is sewn into them (as described for A) before continuing the row. Work well down and level with this hole before making the sewing to avoid a gap forming in the half stitch. The side veins in this pattern are so short that the sewing at the top of the vein is sufficient. Where a longer rib is backed with half stitch (or whole stitch) it will be necessary to sew the runners once or twice in holes in other parts of the vein.

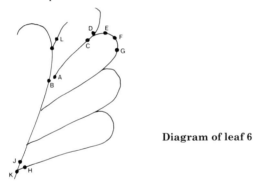

Diagram of leaf 6

LEAF 6: RAISED LEAF WITH TAPS

(See diagram for leaf **6**.) The little sections in this leaf are called 'taps' in Honiton lace. Work the rib forming the centre vein first, sewing in seven pairs and working with the pin holes on the right of the rib. Work the rib right up to the point of the highest central tap. At the third hole from the top, hang in a new pair, bringing it round the pin as usual, but then laying it to the back of the pillow. Make up the edge. Hang in another pair at the next hole, laying it aside with the other new pair. Before working back take the first downright pair past the pin and lay it back next to the other two laid in pairs. The next pin is the topmost one, and after making the edge, turn the pillow.

Work through the first downright pair and tie the runners once. Work the tied runners through all the other downright pairs including the pair which was laid back from the rib and the second of the pairs which were laid in. Leave the runners. Tie the last pair the runners passed through once, and use this pair as new runners to work to the edge. When returning to the rib side, work through all pairs, including the first new pair which was laid in. Leave the runners, tie this pair and use it as new runners to work to the edge.

From now on the runners are top sewn into the rib holes, the first sewing being made into the hole below the one at which the pair was laid in (the fourth hole from the top). Work to the bottom of the tap and take out one pair near the bottom. After the last hole A on the pin hole side, work the runners through to B and sew them there. This last sewing into the rib should always be just below the level of the last hole on the pinhole side.

Tie the sewn runners twice. Put one of the downright pairs on the left aside; open the sewn pair, lift all the other bobbins and lay them down in between the bobbins of the sewn pair. Tie the sewn pair over the bunch twice. Lay aside another pair out of the bunch on the left. Take the bobbins of the bunch in one hand and the tied pair in the other and wind this tied pair round and round the bunched bobbins to make a neat firm roll which should reach up to C. Sew the pair which has done the winding in at D. This is not a top sewing. Insert the needlepin in hole D and bring the point out under the bunch. Draw one of the threads of the winding pair through and put the other through the loop over the bunch. This fastens the roll to the hole.

Tie the sewn pair twice, twist it three times and leave aside to become the edge pair for the next tap. Take the pair which was left out of the bunch and use it to stitch the roll along the side of the first completed tap, by sewing over the roll into each hole after A, as described for the sewing at D. Tie the pair once after each sewing. After sewing into hole C, tie the sewn pair twice and use it as the runner pair to work through the pairs of the roll to the outer side (first having straightened these a little). Twist the runners three times, set pin E under them and hang in a new pair, bringing this round the pin and laying it aside, to be used when filling in the clothwork later. Work the edge stitch with the pair from D. Work a rib across the top of the second tap. * Hang in and lay aside one pair at F, also lay back the pair of downrights nearest the pin before working the next row of rib. Repeat from * at G.

After setting pin G and making the edge, work runners through all pairs, including the pairs that were laid aside, to E. Leave the runners and tie the last pair they worked through, using this pair as new runners. Continue working this tap, making top sewings into the edge of the first tap (over the roll). After the sewing at A, lay in the pair which was left here, to fill the little gap which may appear at this point. The remaining taps on this side are worked similarly.

At the end of each tap the pairs should be reduced to the number needed to make the roll and rib for the next tap and allowing for a pair to fill the gap at the base of the tap. When the last tap has been completed, the threads are rolled up and attached to the centre vein to begin the highest tap on the other side. In this case the rows of weaving are arranged in such a way so that after pin H has been set the runners work to J, where they are sewn and tied twice. The edge pair from H is sewn at K and also tied twice. Bunch the remaining bobbins, cross the sewn pairs under the bunch and tie them over the bunch. Leave one pair behind and make a roll to reach to L, where the rolling pair is sewn in. Use the pair left behind to attach the roll. The second row of taps is worked as the first.

LEAF 7: LADDER TRAIL (OR MITTENS)

This is often indicated on the pattern by a line of widely spaced holes down the centre of a whole stitch leaf. Work three rows, then divide the downrights in half (if there is an odd pair in the middle, add it to the side furthest from the runners). Work the runners through to the middle, twist them three times and leave them. Take the next pair of downrights and use them as runners to work to the other side. Make the edge stitch there and work back to the middle. Twist the runners three times. * Work a whole stitch with the two twisted runner pairs in the middle and twist both pairs three times. The left-hand pair works out to the left edge, the right-hand pair out to the right edge. Make the edge stitches on each side and work both sets of runners back to the middle. Twist both runner pairs three times and repeat from *.

When three or four pinholes of leaf remain, close the ladder trail by working both sets of runners to the middle. Decide which edge hole is to be worked next. If it is a hole on the left, drop the left of the two runner pairs in the middle, and with the right runner pair work through it and onto the left side. If the next edge hole to be worked is on the right, reverse the above, dropping the right pair and work through with the left. The dropped runners become downrights. Continue the braid. The ladder trail tends to become too wide, unless care is taken to pull the downrights on both sides towards the middle after every row.

9 ⣏ Notes on Techniques

NOTE 1: STARTING HONITON BRAID AT A POINT
This occurs when starting leaves, stems, etc.

(a) Whole stitch
Wind knots connecting the pairs a little way back onto one of the bobbins. Hang six pairs round a pin in hole A, so that the knotted threads are in the middle – i.e. the first four bobbins on the left are knot-free and so are the first two bobbins on the right. These are the runners and the two edge pairs. (If B is on the left of A, instead of as shown here, the four knot-free bobbins should be on the outside right and the two on the outside left.) Twist all pairs twice. Take the pair wound with coarse thread, one bobbins in each hand, slip the thread under all central bobbins, omitting the knot-free pairs at the sides, and lay the coarse bobbins to the back of the pillow. Work a whole stitch with the outside pairs on the left, twist both pairs three times and take the inner of these two pairs as runners through all pairs except the last. Twist the runners three times

Starting braid at a point

and set pin B under them. Work a whole stitch with the runners and the edge pair and twist both pairs three times. Bring the coarse threads down into position, to lie third from the left and fifth from the right, making sure that this thread lies inside pin B *.

The coarse thread is treated as a downright and makes a pair with the thread lying inside it. This pair is called the 'coarse pair' and the runners are always worked through it in whole stitch. Continue the braid, using the second pair from the right as runners and working them through all pairs except the last on the left. Twist the runners three times and set pin C under them. Work a whole stitch with the runners and edge pair and twist both pairs three times.

If the space between B and C is a wide one, or if quite a number of new pairs have to be added soon, it is best to start with eight pairs round pin A and this is explained in the first pattern.

(b) Half stitch

Wind the knots further back onto the bobbins, as knots in half stitch are awkward to deal with. Begin exactly as above, working in whole stitch as far as *. Using the inner pair of the two which made the edge stitch at B as runners, ** work a whole stitch through the coarse pair, twist runners once and continue in half stitch through all downright pairs until the coarse pair on the other side is reached. Work a whole stitch through this pair, twist runners three times, set pin C under them and work a whole stitch with the runners and edge pair. Twist both pairs three times. Using the inner of these two pairs as runners, continue from **.

NOTE 2: HANGING IN NEW PAIRS
Always hang in new pairs on the outside of a curve.

(a) In whole stitch braid
After setting the pin and before working the edge stitch, take the new pair, one bobbin in each hand, and slip the thread under the runners. Take both bobbins of the new pair in one hand and slide the thread up the runners and round the pin just set, from the outside in. Lay the new pair inside the coarse thread, or, if no coarse thread is being used, inside the first downright thread, with the knot-free bobbin next to the coarse thread. Complete the edge stitch.

(b) In half stitch braid
Proceed as above but, having laid the new pair inside the coarse thread, twist the inner bobbin of the new pair with the next bobbin on the inside. Complete the edge stitch.

(c) Inside a purl edge
Take the runners to the purl edge. When they have passed through the coarse pair, twist them three times, slip the new pair under them and lay it to the back of the pillow. Complete the purl (note **9**) and, before working the runners back through the coarse pair, bring the new pair from the back of the pillow and lay it inside the coarse thread (twist the inner bobbin of the new pair with the next bobbin on the inside if working in half stitch).

(d) Hanging in two pairs
Normally only one pair is hung in at a time but occasionally, if the space to be filled widens very suddenly, it may be necessary to hang in two pairs at the same pin hole. These may both be hung in as described above, but the following method is also used. Add the first pair in the usual way, make up the edge stitch

and twists and then hang the second pair round the runners (second pair from the edge). Lay this new pair to the back of the pillow and work the runners through to the other side. Before returning, take the new pair from the back of the pillow and lay it inside the coarse thread.

NOTE 3: TAKING OUT PAIRS
Always take out pairs on the inside of a curve.

(a) In whole stitch braid
When the braid narrows and the clothwork becomes too thick, unwanted pairs are simply cut off. Normally the two downrights next to the coarse thread are taken out but if any downrights have knots coming close to the lace, these should be cut off first. Although two threads must be cut off at a time, these need not necessarily be adjacent; as the clothwork is thick, any irregularity in the weaving will not be noticeable.

(b) In half stitch braid
Work towards the side on which a pair is to be taken out until only three pairs remain unworked (i.e. the edge pair, the coarse pair and the pair next to this). Work in *whole stitch* through the next two pairs, before working the usual edge stitch. Take the two bobbins inside the coarse thread (i.e. the two middle bobbins of the two whole stitches), tie them three times close to the lace but not so close that they will force the weaving up, and cut them off. This can be done at either or both ends of the row, wherever it is most convenient or the shape of the braid demands it, provided a whole stitch is worked with the pair inside the coarse thread above the two bobbins to be taken out.

NOTE 4: BACK STITCH
The rows of whole stitch or half stitch should always be at right angles to the lines of pin holes and the work should not be allowed to slope. If it does, a hole on one side must be used more than once, in order to give the other side a chance to catch up. This is done with a back stitch. Work towards the side on which a pin hole is to be used twice. After passing through the coarse pair, twist the runners once and set the pin under them. Do not work the stitch with the edge pair but weave the runners back to the other side and make the usual edge there. Weave runners to the back stitch side and twist them three times after passing through the coarse pair. Remove the pin and replace it into the same hole but under the runners and not into the little loop that it was holding before (this loop tends to disappear as the work progresses). Work the usual edge stitch and three twists (this is called 'making up the back stitch').

When working around a very tight bend, continual back stitching would make the braid too thick and lumpy on the inner edge. In this case, alternate back stitches with working the runners to within the coarse pair on the inner side, leaving them there and working back to the outer edge with the last pair of downrights the runners pass through.

NOTE 5: PREVENTING BRAID PULLING AWAY FROM THE PINS

This tends to happen on the outer side of a sharp curve or corner, resulting in elongated, unsightly pin holes, and can be avoided as follows. Having worked the pin hole at the apex of the curve or corner, take the runners back through the coarse pair and tie them once. Continue with the tied runners to the other side of the braid. The knot keeps the coarse pair up against the pin.

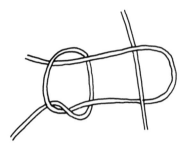

Weaver's knot

NOTE 6: WEAVER'S KNOT

This knot is used for joining short broken threads. Make a slip loop in the end of the thread on the bobbin. Pull the other broken end through this loop until the loop is where you want the knot to be. Take hold of the ends of the slip loop, one in each hand, and pull them apart until the loop has disappeared and the other thread has been pulled into the knot. Test the knot by pulling on the bobbin; if the knot slips off the end of the broken thread, it has not been tied properly – try again.

NOTE 7: GETTING RID OF KNOTS

(a) In whole stitch braid

Simply loop the knotted thread round a pin higher up in the lace so that the knot is in the loop and lay the bobbin back in its position and continue the braid. The loop with the knot in it can be trimmed off later when there is no danger of the thread being pulled out.

(b) In half stitch braid

It is best to avoid knots in half stitch braid, but occasionally a thread does break and a knot has to be coped with. If the thread has broken close to the lace, it is necessary to undo the lace until the end can be tied to the thread on the bobbin, using a weaver's knot (note 6). Continue to undo the lace until the knotted thread is near enough to the end of the row to be taken out in the normal way (note 3b). A new pair will have to be hung in to compensate for the removed pair, unless the braid is becoming narrower. The knot may be further down the thread, where it would become worked into the lace if the thread were allowed to continue in half stitch but where, if the thread were allowed to hang straight down, it would be sewn out or tied out before the knot is reached. In this case, continue working the braid until the knotted thread can be exchanged with the partner of the coarse thread (the coarse pair being the only threads in half stitch which hang straight down).

NOTE 8: LEADWORKS (TALLIES, WOVEN PLAITS, CUTWORKS)

These are much used in Honiton fillings and are always either square or oblong in shape and never have pointed ends, as is the case in some other laces. Two pairs are required, usually twisted several times, according to the filling being worked. Lengthen the second thread from the left and use it as a weaver to weave over the third thread, under and back over the fourth, under the third, over and back under the first. Repeat this sequence of weaving once more, then pull up by gently pulling the weaver whilst holding down the other three bobbins and keeping them slightly spread. Alternate rows of weaving and pulling up until the leadwork is the desired length. The weaver must not be allowed to drop, otherwise the leadwork will be drawn up out of shape. The leadwork can be made wide or narrow, depending on how far apart the outer bobbins are held. The pairs are then twisted again.

NOTE 9: PURLS

Work towards the purl edge, through the coarse pair and twist the runners three times. Work a whole stitch with the runners and edge pair. Twist the outside pair seven times. Take a pin and, holding it with the point towards the braid, place it under the outer thread of the twisted pair. Twist the pin over the thread, towards you and down, and set it into the hole. Twist the second bobbin of the pair round the pin from the outside in, and lay it down inside the outer bobbin. Twist the pair once if the purl is being made on the right-hand side of a braid; for a purl on the left-hand side, the pair is crossed twice, left over right. Work a whole stitch with the edge pair, twist both pairs three times and take the inner pair as runners back into the lace.

NOTE 10: SEWING FORGOTTEN PURLS ONTO AN EDGE

Sew one pair into the hole in the braid previous to the hole in which the purl is needed. Twist seven times, make a purl (note **9**), setting the pin under the braid, into the pin hole in the pricking where the purl is required (take the second bobbin of the pair round the pin from the outside in, and twist once as usual). Sew into the same braid hole and tie once. * Twist seven times to make the next purl, using the next hole in the pricking and at the end sewing into the braid hole. Tie once. Continue from * until all missing purls have been added. Tie three times at the end and cut off.

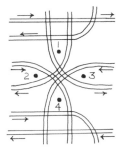

Four pin bud

NOTE 11: FOUR PIN BUD

In whole stitch braid, work until level with top hole 1 and leave runners at edge. Divide downrights in half; if there is an odd pair in the middle, add it to the half nearest the runners. Take runners through to the middle and two pairs more. With the last pair the runners passed through, work back through two pairs. Twist the two middle pairs of these four three times, set pin in hole 1 between them and enclose pin with a whole stitch, twist both pairs three times.

Use the two outer pairs of the four middle pairs as runners and take each to its respective edge; make the edge stitches (or, more likely, a back stitch) and work back to the middle, leaving the twisted middle pairs unworked. Twist each runner pair three times and set pins 2 and 3 under them. With each runner pair and the nearest of the two twisted middle pairs work a whole stitch and twist all four pairs three times. Again use the two outer pairs of the four middle pairs as runners to work to the edges; make edge stitches (or back stitches) and work back again to the middle, leaving the two twisted middle pairs unworked. With these two twisted middle pairs work a whole stitch, twist both pairs three times and set pin in hole 4 between them. Do not enclose this pin.

Decide which edge hole is to be worked next; if it is at the right edge, take the right-hand runners through the remaining three middle pairs to the left. If the next hole to be worked is at the left edge, take the left-hand runners through the remaining three middle pairs to the right. Leave the runners, and use the last pair they worked through as runners to work to the edge at which the next hole is to be worked; make the edge stitch, and continue the braid. The other runners stay where they are and become downrights.

NOTE 12: WINDOWS

Worked in whole stitch braid. This is a line of small holes across the entire width of a whole stitch braid, sometimes used as a vein in a leaf or flower. The braid should be fairly open, with not too many downrights in it, otherwise the windows will not show up well. Work the runners through the coarse pair, twist them three times and * work a whole stitch with the next pair. Twist both pairs three times. Continue from * until runners arrive at the coarse pair, on the other side. This should not be twisted. Finish the row as usual. In the next row, only the runner pair is twisted three times after each stitch. The downrights are not twisted.

NOTE 13: SMALL HOLE IN WHOLE STITCH BRAID

Work the runners to where the hole is needed. Twist the runners and the last pair they passed through three times. Work a whole stitch with the next down-right pair and twist this three times, but do not twist the runners. Work runners on to the edge. In the next row, the runners only are twisted three times, immediately below the three twists made by the runners in the last row. Continue the braid.

NOTE 14: SNATCH-PIN HOLE WITH LEADWORK IN WHOLE STITCH BRAID

This usually consists of eight or ten pin holes pricked in a circle. Work until level with the top snatch-pin hole and leave runners at the edge. Divide down-rights in half; if there is an odd pair in the middle, add it to the half nearest the runners. Work the runners through to the middle and one pair more and leave. With the last pair which the runners passed through, work back through two pairs. With the two middle pairs of these four make a whole stitch, twist each pair three times, set pin A between them and enclose the pin with a whole stitch but do not twist. Using these two pairs as runners, work the left pair out to the left edge and the right pair out to the right edge, make up the edge stitches, and work back to the middle.

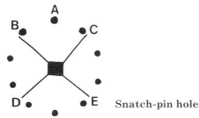

Snatch-pin hole

Twist both runner pairs seven times and set pins under them into holes B and C. Work out to the edges (back stitching if necessary) and back again to the middle, leaving the last downright pair on each side unworked (to be used for the leadwork later). Twist the runners seven times and set pins under them on each side. The runners continue to work out to the edges and back to the middle, twisting seven times round the snatch pins and back stitching, if necessary, on the outer edges to keep the work level.

No hole on the outer edges should be worked below the level of the snatch-pin hole, otherwise gaps will appear around the hole on each side. Continue until only the last three holes of the snatch-pin hole are unworked and leave. Twist each of the pairs left hanging from pins B and C three or four times, depending on the size of the hole, make a small, square leadwork with them and twist them three or four times again. Work the runners through these two pairs before twisting and setting pins D and E under them. Work both runners to the edges again and back to the centre, twist one runner pair seven times and set a pin under it into the last hole, but do not enclose the pin. Take the other runners through this pair (which now become downrights) to the other edge. Continue the normal braid.

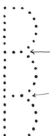

Crossing the coarse threads

NOTE 15: CROSSING THE COARSE THREADS

A pin hole in the middle of the braid often denotes that the coarse threads are to be crossed. This is done to make a division in the braid, or to separate areas of whole stitch and half stitch. Work the braid until the holes on both sides of the central hole have been made up. When one side of the braid is straight and the other curved, arrange the stitches so that the leaders can be left on the curved side.

Lengthen the coarse thread on the curved side and weave it through the downrights, round the coarse thread on the other side and back through the downrights to its original position. It is always best to begin the weaving by taking the coarse thread over its neighbour and under the next thread. Pull up the weaving thread by pulling it against the other coarse thread, which should be held taut in the other hand. Shorten the coarse thread again and continue the braid, tying the runners once after they have passed through the coarse pair, to keep this up in position.

NOTE 16: CROSSING ONE BRAID OVER ANOTHER

Work the braid to where it has to cross an already completed part. After making up the last hole, work one more row. Sew the runners and edge pairs into appropriate holes of the completed braid, tying them three times. Bunch the bobbins, cross the two sewn edge pairs under the bunch and tie them three times over the bunch. The tied edge pairs and one other pair are then sewn into appropriate holes on the other side of the completed braid, the bobbins are more or less disentangled, and the braid is continued in the usual way.

NOTE 17: DIVIDING A BRAID INTO TWO

Work until level with the top hole of the division, and leave the runners at one edge. Do not work any edge holes below the level of this top hole – if necessary leave a back stitch at one edge to avoid this. Sort out the two middle pairs of downrights, pushing the other bobbins a little way away on each side. Take one of the outer bobbins of the two middle pairs and lay it with the bobbins of the nearest side section. Take the innermost bobbin of the other side section and lay it with the three bobbins remaining in the middle. There are now two pairs in the middle and an odd number of bobbins in each side section. Take a new pair wound with coarse thread and weave the thread through the two middle pairs. Lay this pair to the back of the pillow.

With the two middle pairs work a whole stitch and twist both pairs three times. Work the runners from the edge through the bobbins of the nearest side section, bringing down the nearest coarse thread from the back of the pillow to join the odd bobbin at the end of the section. Work the runners through this pair, twist them three times and set a pin under them into the top hole of the division. Hang a new pair round the runners, laying it to the back of the pillow (this will be needed later as runner pair for the other branch); make a whole stitch with the runners and the nearest twisted middle pair. Twist both pairs three times.

Continue this branch of the braid, bring down the other coarse thread from the back of the pillow to lie in between the other side section and the remaining twisted middle pair. If the second branch is not to be worked for some time, it is advisable to lengthen these threads so that the bobbins hang over the side of the pillow, with one of the cover cloths pinned over them. Be careful when handling the pillow not to snap these bobbins off.

When returning to the second branch of the braid, bring down the pair which was hung in earlier and work it as runner pair to the outer edge. Work back to the inner side, using the remaining twisted middle pair as edge pair.

NOTE 18: RIB (TEN-STICK, STEM STITCH)

This has pin holes on one side only and can be made with any number of pairs from four to about eight pairs. If the line of holes is curved, work the rib with the pin holes on the outer side of the curve. Set a pin in the first hole and hang the pairs round it, twist all pairs twice, or sew the required number of pairs into an already completed part of the work (in which case do not twist). Work a whole stitch with the two outer pairs on the pin hole side and twist both pairs three times. * Work the inner of these two pairs to the plain side through all pairs. Twist the runners once and leave them. Work the last pair the runners passed through as new runners to the pin hole side through all pairs except the last. Twist the runners three times, set the pin in the next hole under them, make the usual edge stitch, and twist each pair three times. Repeat from *. After setting the last pin, work the runners to the plain side and sew out as usual.

An alternative method of making the plain edge is to work the runners from the pin hole side through all pairs to the plain side, then make a second stitch with the runners and the last pair they passed through. The inner pair of these two then works back to the pin hole side.

NOTE 19: CROSSING ONE RIB OVER ANOTHER

Take the runners to the plain side, sew them into the nearest hole of the rib to be crossed, and tie them once. Sew the edge pair on the other side into the next or next but one hole (depending on the width of the rib being worked) of the rib being crossed, tie them once, and twist them three times. Continue the rib by taking the runners from the plain side through the passives and working the next pin hole.

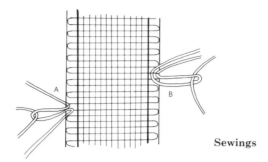

Sewings

NOTE 20: SEWINGS

(a) Ordinary sewings

When the work in progress has to be joined into an already completed part, this is done by means of 'sewings'. These are made by drawing one of the pair of threads to be joined through an edge hole of the completed braid to form a loop, passing the other bobbin of the pair through this loop, and pulling up both threads. Remove the pin from the edge hole of the completed braid, to which the join is to be made. Insert a needlepin into this braid hole, and bring the point of the needlepin out under the edge of the braid. Press one of the threads of the pair to be joined under the needle point and manoeuvre this back into the hole in the pricking, taking a loop of the thread with it. Holding the bobbin so that this thread is quite taut, slowly draw the needlepin out of the hole, and at the same time bend the handle end down. At the last moment, slacken the thread, and flick the needle point out of the hole and through the hole in the braid, and the loop of thread should come out with it. Pass the other bobbin through this loop and pull up. Replace the pin. It is important to make the sewing into the pin hole and not into the space between two pin holes. Sewings require some practice before they can be made easily.

(b) Top sewings or raised sewings

These are used mainly for raised work, or where a particularly close join is required, or when sewing out fillings, when the cut ends of threads are not so likely to show on the right side, as in an ordinary sewing. This sewing is made round one of the little side bars of the pin hole. Insert the needlepin into the pin hole to which the sewing is to be made, and bring the point of the needle out from under the side bar. Draw one of the pairs of threads through and complete as for an ordinary sewing.

(c) Sewing in new pairs into a completed braid

This is used for fillings, or to work another adjoining piece of braid. Insert the needlepin into the pin hole of the completed braid and bring the point out under the edge. Press the thread connecting the new pair under the needle point, take both bobbins of the new pair into one hand and lift them, so that the needlepin can be slid into the hole in the pricking with a loop of thread. Bring the loop of thread through and put one of the pair of bobbins through it. Pull up both bobbins. Replace the pin in the pin hole. When sewing in pairs for fillings, it is sometimes found that the pin holes are not placed in exactly the positions in which the pairs are wanted. In this case, after sewing into the nearest pin hole, the pair may be tied once, pulling it to the left or right of the pin hole (whichever is required), before tightening the knot.

(d) Sewing out pairs from a filling

The pairs are sewn into the completed braid as described above (**20b**), after which they are tied three times each and laid back to be cut off later, when all the pairs from the filling have been sewn out. If necessary, more than one pair can be sewn into the same hole in the braid.

When sewing out the pairs which have made a leadwork, sew out the pair which contains the weaver first, if this is possible, pulling the thread which is not the weaver through to make the loop, then passing the weaver through this loop carefully, and pull up. Then sew out the other pair.

(e) Sewings where two rows of pin holes meet

When the braid being worked approaches close to an already completed braid, the two should be joined, even though each has its own edge holes. When the pin has been set, and the edge stitch made, do not twist the pairs. Remove the pin from the hole in the adjacent braid in which the join is to be made, and sew the edge pair to it. Now work a whole stitch with the other runners, twist both pairs three times and continue working after replacing the pin.

(f) Sewing into a hole in which braid was started at a point

Since several loops hang round this pin, the pin hole would be lost if the pin were removed for the sewing. Therefore the sewing should be made with the pin in position. Insert the needlepin close by the pin and bring it out under the loops held by the pin. Complete the sewing in the usual way.

(g) Sewings to attach a roll to a completed edge

When a roll has been made in raised work, a pair is usually left out of the roll and used to attach the roll to each hole of a completed edge. Remove the pin from the first hole. Insert the needlepin into the hole, and bring it out under the completed edge and under the roll, and hook through one of the threads of the sewing pair. Complete the sewing in the usual way. Tie the sewing pair once and replace the pin. Repeat this process up the roll, and tie the sewing pair twice after the last sewing.

NOTE 21: LAYING IN PAIRS FOR SUBSEQUENT USE

When the part being worked passes the place where the next braid will later begin, it is possible to hang in the pairs which will be needed for the braid, and so save having to sew them in. They can be hung on the runners at the holes above the section to be worked later, both before and after the edge stitch has been made, and laid aside. This is not always practicable, and can only be decided by studying the pattern.

NOTE 22: ADDING THE COARSE PAIR WHEN NOT STARTING AT A POINT

When starting a piece of braid for which the pairs are sewn in or laid in previously, the coarse pair must be woven through the downrights and placed to the back of the pillow, until the first row has been worked to keep it in place. An alternative way is to hang the coarse pair round a pin above the piece to be worked and lay it in position immediately. The ends of the coarse thread can be cut off when the section is completed.

NOTE 23: SEWING OUT A BRAID

(a) Sewing out a braid into a braid

When the last edge hole has been worked, take the runners back through all pairs except the runners on the other side. This final row is always worked in whole stitch, even when it follows half stitch braid. Lay back the coarse threads. The pairs are now sewn into an already completed part of the work. Two or even three pairs may be sewn into each hole of the completed braid. The runners and edge pairs should always be sewn and as many pairs as possible in between. Tie all sewn and unsewn pairs three times. Bunch the bobbins, cross the two sewn outer pairs under the bunch and tie them three times over the bunch – i.e. take one bobbin from each pair, tie them three times, then take the other bobbin from each pair and tie them. Cut off all pairs, using the method described in note **25**. If the braid being sewn out is very wide, it is better to form two bunches, making sure that the pairs which are crossed under and tied over the bunches are sewn pairs. Trim off all the ends of thread and the coarse threads close to the lace, taking care not to cut into the knots.

(b) To sew out a braid or a rib into a rib

After the last pin hole and the final row have been worked, only the edge pairs and runners are sewn and tied – the downright pairs should be tied without sewing and the pairs are bunched and cut off in the normal way. If desired, one of the pairs which were thrown out before the sewing out began, may be used to tie back the bunch of threads over the braid. No ends should be seen when the lace is turned over. With experience, it is possible to tie the sewn pairs so well back into the pin hole loop that when bunched and cut off the ends do not show.

When a rib is sewn out after the last pin is set, work to the plain side, then sew out and tie runners, the pair next to them and the edge pair on the pin hole side. Cut out two pairs of downrights from the centre of the rib, tie the remaining pairs, and bunch and tie as usual.

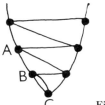
Finishing at a point

NOTE 24: FINISHING A BRAID AT A POINT

Cut out pairs as the braid narrows. Lay aside two pairs on one side near the end (inside the coarse thread at pins A and B in the diagram); these will be wanted again. After setting pin C and making the edge stitch, cut out the coarse threads and take the runners through all remaining pairs, including the edge pair on the other side (without twisting). Tie all pairs three times, beginning with the runners.

Bunch the bobbins, cross the outside pairs under the bunch and tie them three times over the bunch. Remove every alternate pin and push the remainder down into the pillow, leaving the last two or three on each side standing. The two pairs which were laid aside must now be spread out, so that one bobbin of each pair lies on each side of the lace. Turn all the bunched bobbins back over the lace between the standing pins and tie the spread pairs three times over the bunch. Cut off.

NOTE 25: BOWING OFF

Honiton bobbins are usually cut off from the pillow and tied together ready for the next piece of work in one action, using a pair of small, blunt scissors with points. Hold the pair to be cut off loosely in one hand and place the pair of scissors – points closed – under the pair of threads to be cut off. Twist the point of the scissors over the thread, towards you and down, so that a loop of thread forms round the scissors. Open the scissors and catch the thread running from the scissors to the lace between the blades from underneath. Close the scissors (if they are blunt enough they should not cut the threads) and move the bobbins towards the lace, still holding them so that the threads are quite slack, until the loop slides off the points of the scissors, a new loop is held in the blades and a knot is formed. Tighten the knot by pulling the thread between the bobbins and the top loop taut, open the scissors and cut the loop. Pull the bobbins away – they will be found to be tied. If there are knots in the threads to be cut off or on the bobbins, where they will soon work out, it is best to unwind the bobbins, so that the pairs can be bowed off below the knots, which are left behind on the threads to be trimmed off from the lace.

NOTE 26: PINNING DOWN THE COMPLETED LACE

When a section is finished, or when the pins begin to get in the way of the part being worked, every other pin can be removed and the remainder pushed right down into the pillow. When doing this, while the work is still in progress, leave at least 1 cm ($\frac{1}{2}$ in.) of pins standing on each side of the part being worked.

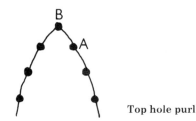

Top hole purl

NOTE 27: STARTING A LEAF WITH A PURL AT THE TOP HOLE

Hang six pairs and the coarse pair, as usual at pin A, which in this case is the first hole at the side of the leaf. Work across to the top hole (B) and make a purl. Tie back the coarse pair (note **5**) and work to A again. Gently take out the pin, make the purl in A and tie the runners well back against the coarse pair again. Continue working as normal, adding new pairs.

NOTE 28: RUBBINGS

This is a convenient way of obtaining copies of prickings. Lay the pricking, wrong or rough side uppermost, on a table, place a piece of thin paper (copy paper, airmail writing paper, etc.) over it and, holding this down firmly, rub lightly over the pattern with a piece of heelball. This can be obtained from a shoe repair shop or from a shop selling artists' materials (as it is also used for brass rubbings). The pin holes from the pricking will be transferred onto the paper.

NOTE 29: MARKINGS ON PATTERNS

Occasionally odd holes are found on Honiton prickings and it is useful to know their meaning. Two holes close together in the middle of a braid mean that this portion is to be worked in half stitch. Four holes, grouped as for a four pin bud and pricked on the card outside the pattern, indicate where purls should be made. This is often accompanied by a line scratched on the pattern outside the outer holes to another group of four holes, showing the extent of the purl edge. A single hole between the two edges of the braid shows where the coarse thread crosses, or may also indicate a hole (for an eye, nail, etc.). Which of these is intended can usually be seen by studying the pattern. A line of widely spaced holes indicates a twisted vein, ladder trail or windows.

NOTE 30: WORKING THREADS FROM ONE SECTION TO ANOTHER

First method

Work to 1 and make a back stitch at this hole. Work to 2 and sew the runner pair and the edge pairs at this hole. Tie the edge pair three times at this hole and lay aside to be cut off later. With the sewn runners work through one pair. Tie the runners once and work them through two more pairs. * Leave the runners and with the last pair they work through, work back to hole 3. Sew the

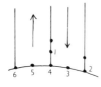

a   **Working threads from one section to another**

runners here. Take the two bobbins inside the coarse bobbin or, if a coarse thread is not being used, inside the first bobbin, tie them three times and cut them out. Work the sewn runners again through three pairs, and repeat from * twice (holes 4 and 5). From 5 the sewn runners are taken through all down-rights to 1, to make up the back stitch there. Work to 6 and sew the runners there. Tie the runners once, twist them three times and leave them to become an edge pair. The threads are now in position to work the adjoining section. Take the edge pairs left at 1 as runners out to the outer edge and work the next pin hole there. Continue the next section taking sewings on the inner side.

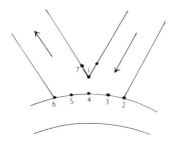

b

Second method
Sometimes the two sections are not joined as above. In this case, work as above until the runners have been sewn at 6. Work the sewn runners to 7 and make the edge stitch there. Before returning, sew a new pair at 6, twist it three times and use it as the new edge pair on this side.

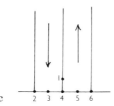

c

Third method
In this turning there is no completed edge to which the runners can be sewn and the lower edge 2 – 6 must be made at the same time as the turn. Work to 1 and make a backstitch at this hole. Work to 2 and make the edge stitch. Work through the coarse pair, tie the runners and work through two more pairs. ** Leave the runners and use the last pair they worked through as new runners to work to 3, where they make the edge stitch. Take the two bobbins inside the coarse thread, tie them three times and cut them off. Work back through three pairs and repeat from ** for holes 4 and 5 (do not take out a pair at 5). From 5

the runners work through to 1 to make up the back stitch there. Work to 6. Untwist the inner edge pair and weave the coarse thread between these two bobbins to lie as the thread next to the sewing edge. Continue the next section, after tying the runners at 6, and take sewings on the inner side.

These are general methods and must be adapted to suit each individual pattern. The number of pin holes along the base line may vary according to the width of the piece being turned and there may not be enough pairs to enable one to throw out a pair at the last hole or two of the turn. On the other hand, if there are too many pairs, making the clothwork too thick round the back stitch, one or two extra pairs may be taken out before the back stitch is made up.

Starting at the head of a scroll

NOTE 31: STARTING AT THE HEAD OF A SCROLL

If the scroll is not too sharply turned, start towards the outer side of the head (see diagram **a**) where a number of back stitches on the inner side will make it possible to get around without the use of any other method.

Remember to tie the runners (note **5**) several times along the outside of the curve. If the scroll is sharply turned, proceed according to diagram **b**. Set up with eight pairs and a coarse pair, and work back and forth in the usual way, hanging in new pairs on the outside of the curve immediately; at hole A work a back stitch, which is not made up until the head of the scroll is turned. From A work to the outer side, make the edge stitch there and work back through three pairs only (i.e. the coarse pair and two more pairs). Leave the runners and take the last pair they worked through as new runners to the outer edge again where the next hole is worked. Bring the runners back through the coarse pair and leave them. Take the nearest of the downright pairs which were unworked in the previous row (the sixth pair counting from the outer side) in whole stitch to the outer edge.

* Make the next edge stitch, take the runners back through the coarse pair and leave them. Take the next of the unworked downright pairs in whole stitch to the outer edge and repeat from * until all the downright pairs except the inner coarse pair have been worked to the outer edge. If the head of the scroll is wide, it will be necessary to add several new pairs on the outer side while the turn is being made. Finally, the back stitch at A is made up, and the braid is continued normally. Several pairs will have to be taken out on the inside as the scroll narrows.

GENERAL NOTES

Honiton lace is always made with the wrong side upwards. The fact that this lace has a wrong side limits its use, but it has the advantage that, having finished one part, the threads can be finished off neatly and taken across the lace already made to work the next part, without cutting the threads off.

Once the basic stitches have been mastered, the worker should watch the lace and not the bobbins, so as to be able to detect mistakes at once.

Always set pins in the pin holes slanting slightly outwards and backwards, otherwise the lace becomes longer than the pattern, the tension tends to become loose, and the lace will gradually rise from the pattern instead of remaining flat.

Pull the runners up well at the end of each row, work the first stitch through the coarse pair and again pull well – this will help to make small, neat pin holes.

Always keep the coarse threads close to the pins, and do not move the coarse bobbins unnecessarily across the pillow.

Do not lift the bobbins above the surface of the pillow.

Keep all threads and bobbins of similar length when working, about 8 to 10 cm (3 or 4 in.) of thread between bobbin and lace. The bobbins can then glide over each other and need no lifting.

Keep the pattern to be worked facing you, and move all the bobbins, except the coarse bobbins, well to obtain good tension.

Always twist bobbins right over left, hence, if one has to unpick to rectify mistakes, it is automatic to untwist left over right. The only exception to this rule is when making a left-hand purl (see note **9**).

Do not wind too much thread onto the bobbins.

Study the pattern well before beginning the work: usually a flower, main stem or section must be worked first, so that other parts may be worked and attached to it. If you do not follow the correct order of working, you will have to put bobbins aside, until the main section has been worked.

When starting a ladder trail or twisted vein, twist the runners once in the first row, twice in the next row, and then continue with three twists. Reverse this process to close the vein – the start and finish will be much neater.

Remember, when working a purl edge, that fewer pairs will be needed, so take out one or two pairs according to the width of the section being worked.

Some pricking card tends to be rather hard to prick; it can be softened and made more pliable if it is slightly warmed.

A good lacemaker should be able to use her patterns several times. Place a double piece of writing paper under the pattern after the first use. This will hold the pins firm where there are any worn or enlarged holes. On the other hand, it is false economy to use any pattern too often, as small particles of card can get worked into the lace and are difficult to remove.

Always cover the pillow with a cover cloth when it is not in use.

Do not handle threads more than necessary. The needlepin should be used to lengthen or shorten threads. To shorten threads, insert the point of the needlepin into the loop of the hitch on the bobbin. Pull the loop away from the bobbin and wind the bobbin towards you, easing the loop with the needlepin as you wind. When lengthening the bobbin, the thread sometimes becomes caught behind other threads and can be loosened with the needlepin in the same way.

When starting a leaf, an experienced worker will tie the runners after passing through the coarse pair, after each of the first two pins have been set. This results in neater pin holes at the top. This also applies when starting a braid for which pairs have been sewn or laid in.

Always keep lace and thread in blue paper, and away from daylight, to keep it white and clean.

Bibliography

Treadwin, *Antique Point and Honiton Lace*, (Ward Lock & Tyler, London, first published 1874)

Devonia, *The Honiton Lace Book*, (The Bazaar Office, London, first published 1873; reprinted by Paul Minet, London, 1972)

Maidment, Margaret, *A Manual of Handmade Bobbin Lace*, (Charles T Branford Co, Boston, 1954; reprinted by Piccadilly Rare Books, Paul Minet, London)

Nottingham, Pamela, *The Technique of Bobbin Lace*, (B T Batsford, London; Van Nostrand Reinhold, New York)

Penderel Moody, A., *Devon Pillow Lace*, (Cassell & Co Ltd, first published 1907)

Wright, Doreen, *Bobbin Lace Making*, (G Bell & Co, London, 1971)

List of Suppliers

UK
Mace & Nairn
89 Crane Street
Salisbury SP1 2PY
Wiltshire

A Sells
Lane Cove
49 Pedley Lane
Clifton, Shefford, Beds

D J Hornsby
149 High Street
Burton Latimer
Kettering, Northants

Honiton Lace Shop
44 High Street
Honiton
Devon

USA
Frederick J Fawcett Inc
129 South Street
Boston, Mass 02111
(linen yarns)

Some Place
2990 Adeline Street
Berkeley, California 94703
(yarns, bobbins, cushions)

Osma Galliger Tod
319 Mendoza Avenue
Coral Gables, Florida 33134
(yarns, bobbins, cusions)

Robin and Russ Handweavers
533 N. Adams Street
McMinnville, Oregon 97128
(books, materials and equipment)

Index